Physical Handicap

Designed and produced by
Aladdin Books Ltd
70 Old Compton Street
London W1V 5PA

First published in
Great Britain in 1990 by
Franklin Watts Ltd
96 Leonard Street
London EC2A 4RH

Editor: Roger Vlitos
Editorial Planning: Clark Robinson Ltd
Design: David West
Children's Book Design
Illustrator: Ian Moores
Picture Research: Cecilia Weston-Baker

ISBN 0-7496-0101-9

Printed in Belgium

The publishers wish to acknowledge that the photographs reproduced within this book have been posed by models or have been obtained from photographic agencies.

A CIP catalogue record for this book is available from the British Library.

CONTENTS

Living with

Physical Handicap

Dr John Shenkman

FRANKLIN WATTS
London : New York : Toronto : Sydney

WHAT IS A PHYSICAL HANDICAP ?

A physical handicap is any kind of disability or disease that puts the person who has it at a disadvantage compared to most other people. Of course we are all ill from time to time with a sore throat or influenza; we may even have to take some time off school as a result. A physical handicap, however, has a more permanent effect on the sufferer's life. Special effort has to be made to live with the problems that a physical handicap presents.

Every human body is made up of tiny units called cells which grow together to form skin, nerves, blood, bone, etc. These all belong to a complex set of inter-related systems (see the diagrams below). Each system depends on the others to help it function properly. Our skeletons, muscles, blood, organs and nerves all combine to make us function normally. If any one thing goes seriously wrong it may result in the condition we call physical handicap.

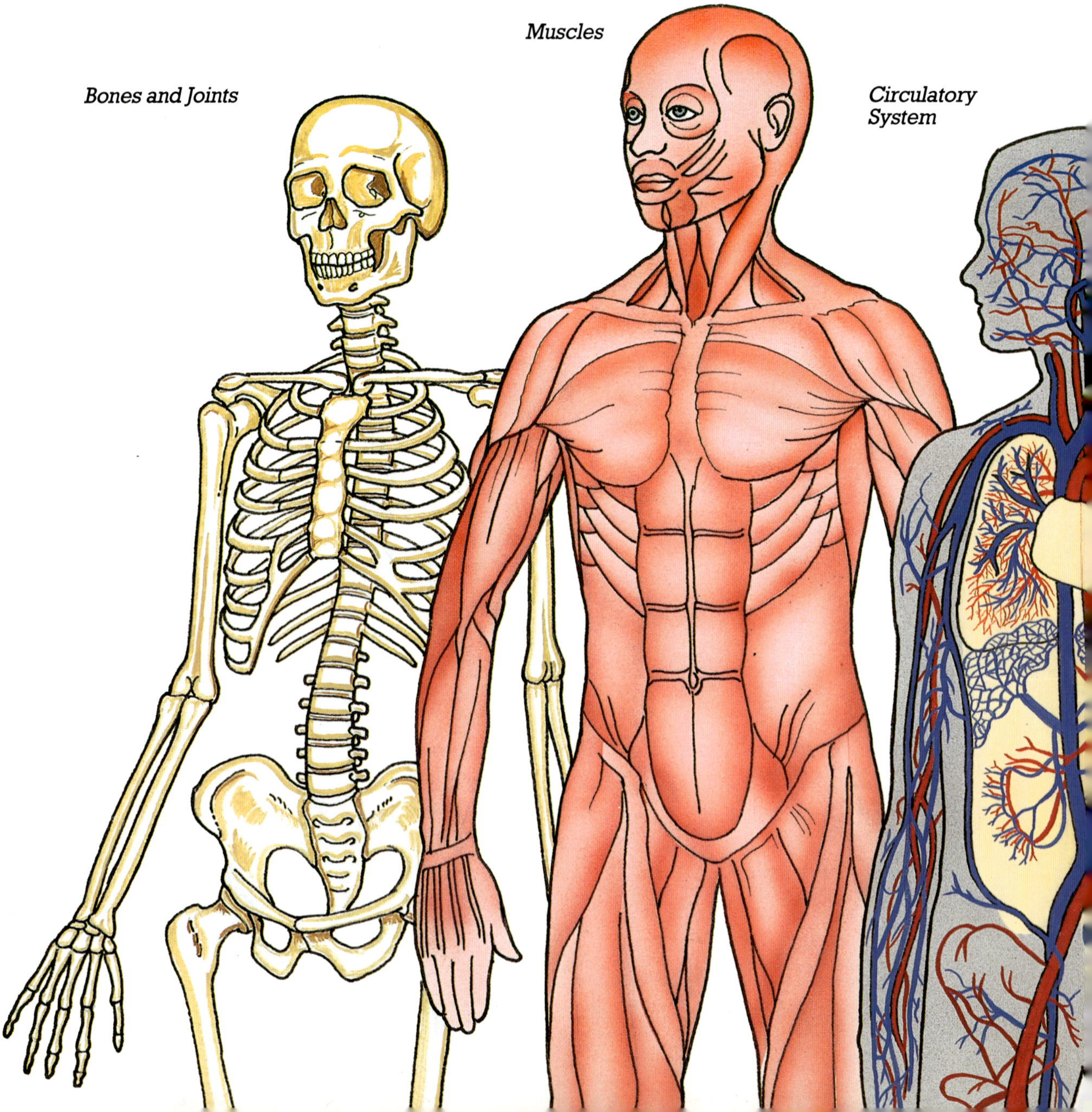

Social implications

Some physical handicaps can prevent a person from doing all the things that able-bodied people do. For instance, we presume all children will run, skip, shout, sing and have plenty of spare energy. But if someone is afflicted by a physical handicap they may well not be able to manage the things which are normal for most people. This does not mean that they have to be socially handicapped as well. Many disabled people excel in unexpected ways. Professor Stephen W. Hawking of Cambridge University has been wheelchair-bound for the past 20 years and has lost the ability to speak. Nevertheless, he is the world leader in his field and, with the aid of a computer, he delivers lectures and writes books. A disability need not become a social handicap – both the sufferer and society can work together to overcome the obstacles it presents.

Physical implications

Serious damage to any of the systems illustrated in the diagrams below will result in a loss of some physical ability. If the skeleton, joints or muscles are harmed the result may be problems with walking, running, playing games, or climbing stairs. If the heart, lungs or blood circulation are impaired a person will not be able to do strenuous exercise without becoming short of breath and tiring quickly. Damage to the brain or nervous system can alter the way the mind controls the muscles, and so affect the body's movements. Even the digestive system can suffer from diseases which will lead to physical handicap – if the lining of the gut is ulcerated or scarred because of a disease, nutrients cannot be absorbed from food.

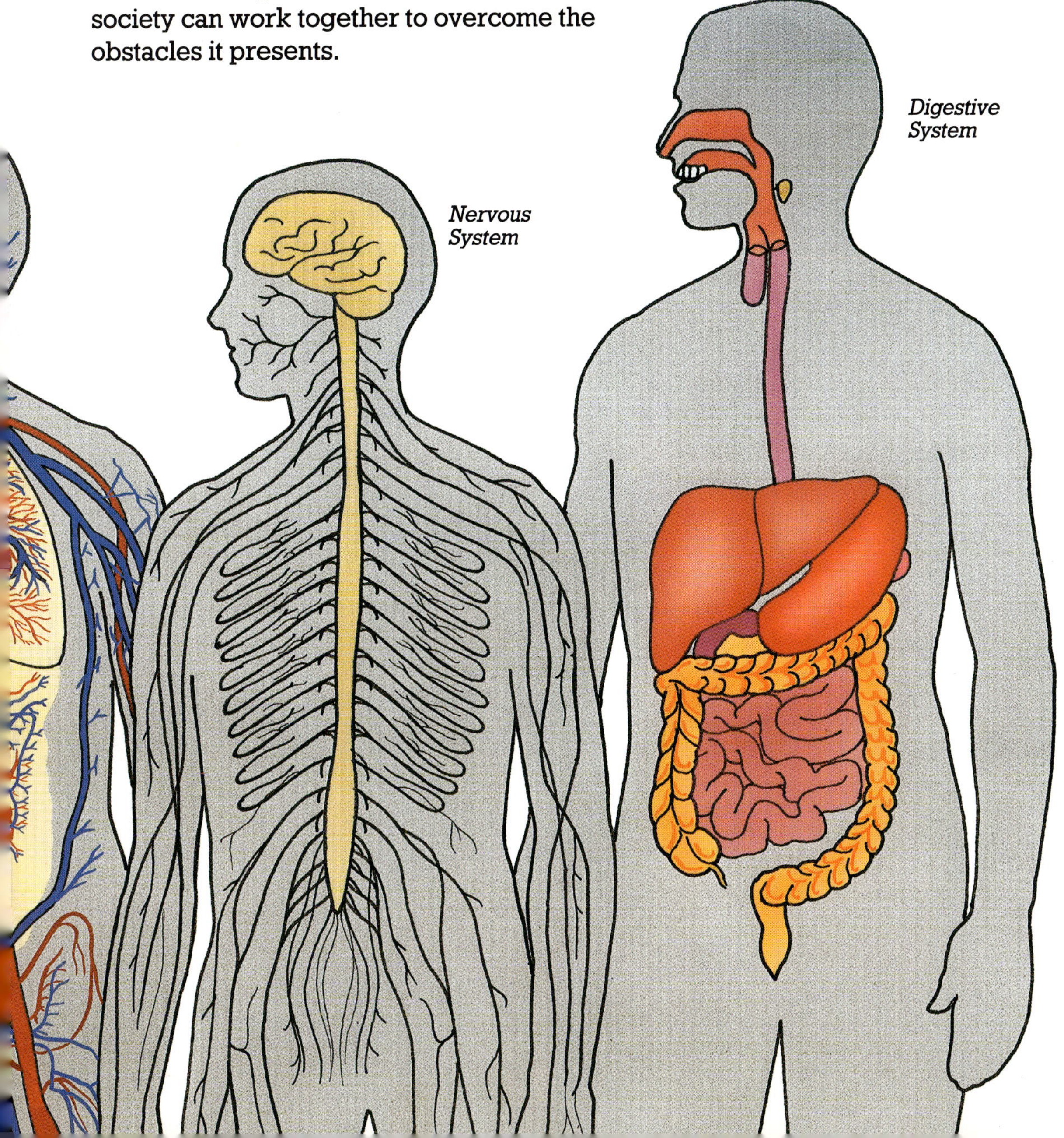

WHAT GOES WRONG ?

Many physical disabilities are caused by damage to the body's nervous system. To understand why, it helps to have a look at how it works. The illustrations below show a brain, the top of a spinal cord and a typical nerve cell. Certain areas of the brain control special functions. Hearing, memory and sight, for instance, each have their own portion. The cerebellum coordinates and smooths our muscular movements.

The brain is like a computer which receives messages from the rest of the body about the world outside. It sorts through masses of information every second and sends signals to the performing parts of the body telling them what to do. Both these initial messages to the brain (via sensory nerves) and the brain's instructions to the body (via motor nerves) are passed along the nerves as tiny electrical impulses. A disorder of the nerve cells will destroy these lines of communication. This, in turn, may result in a physical handicap.

THE BRAIN

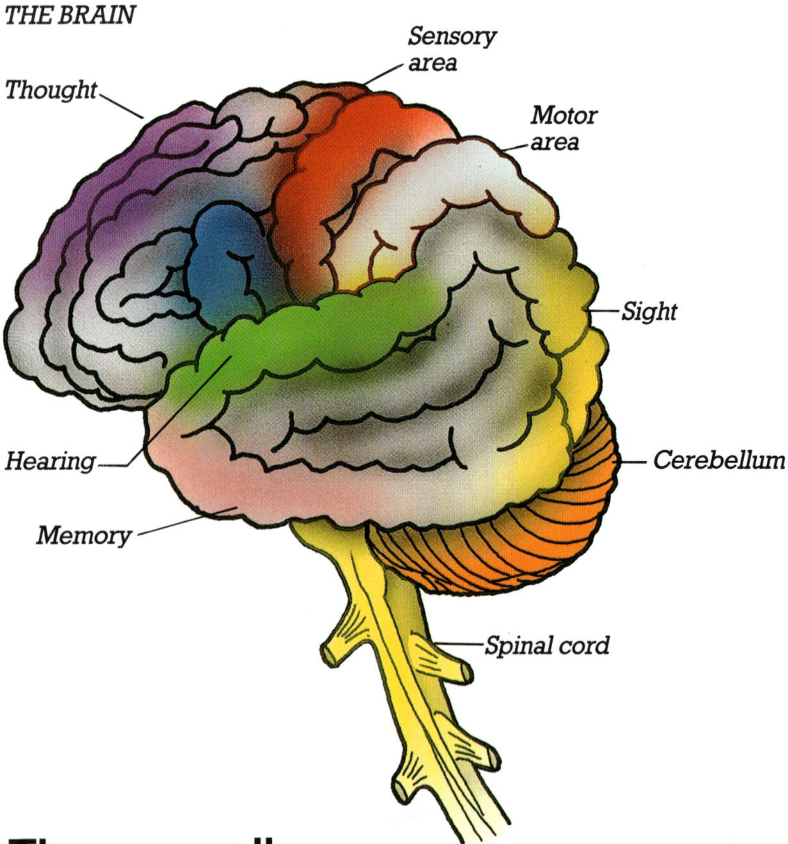

SENSORY NERVE CELL

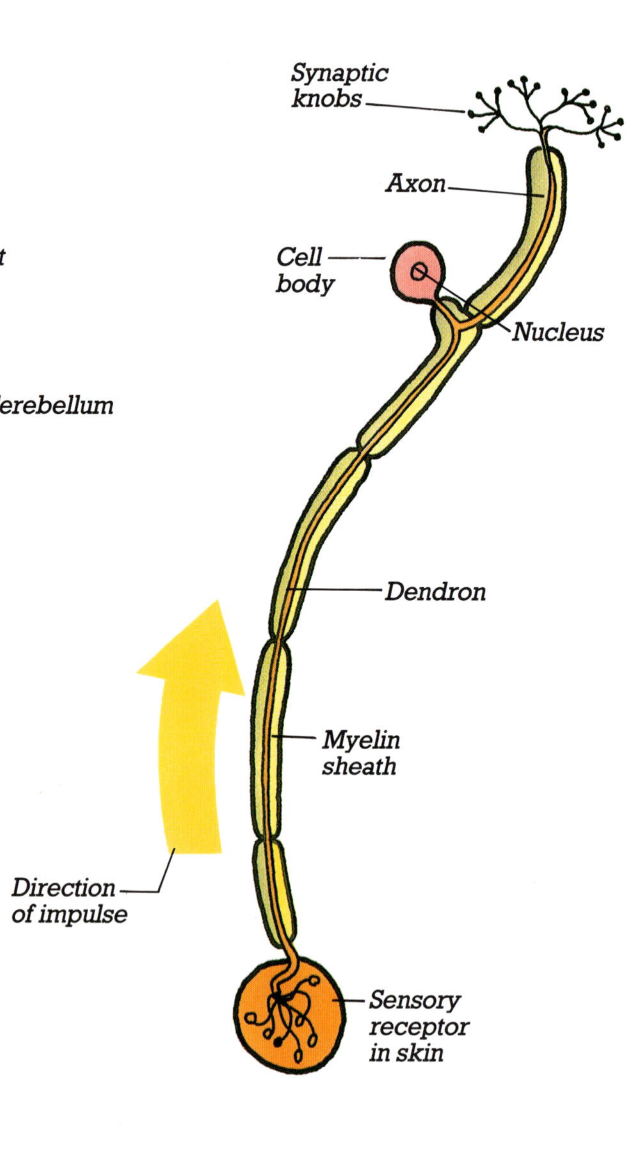

The nerve cell

The nervous system is made up of thousands of millions of nerve cells. An example of a sensory nerve cell is illustrated on the right of this page. It consists of a cell body with a nucleus, and a dendron or branch-like connection of dendrites. These conduct nerve impulses towards the cell body. The axon conducts impulses away from the cell.

Multiple sclerosis

Multiple sclerosis, or M.S. as it is commonly called, is a distressing disease which attacks the nervous system. M.S. is simple to understand if you know how normal nerve impulses operate within the body. The diagrams below show that a nerve fibre consists of a thin central thread surrounded by long "sausages" of myelin sheath. Between each of these sausages is a tiny gap. Electrical impulses are conducted along the nerve by exchanges of chemical salts across these gaps. The nerve impulse starts at the synapse of the dendron and ends at the synapse of the axon. Synapses are the sensitive nerve cells where signals are exchanged. Impulses start at the sensory receptor, which might be a taste-bud in your tongue or the nerve ending on a fingertip. The electrical impulses pass up to your brain via two successive nerves and their synapse. As a result of this process the brain becomes aware of taste or feel. In motor nerves the impulses pass in the opposite direction from those in a sensory nerve cell. They pass across the motor end-plate and stimulate the muscle fibres to move.

In M.S. the myelin sheaths surrounding the thread-like axon are destroyed. When these are lost, nerve impulses can no longer be conducted. Some healing may occur, but scar tissue develops and interferes with nerve function. The nerve cell itself may even die. As this disease progresses it can affect the brain as well as sensory and motor cells. It can cause stiff limbs, loss of vision, loss of balance, unsteadiness of movement and bladder problems. Continued destruction over the years leads to severe physical handicap. This disease has long periods of remission and recurrence.

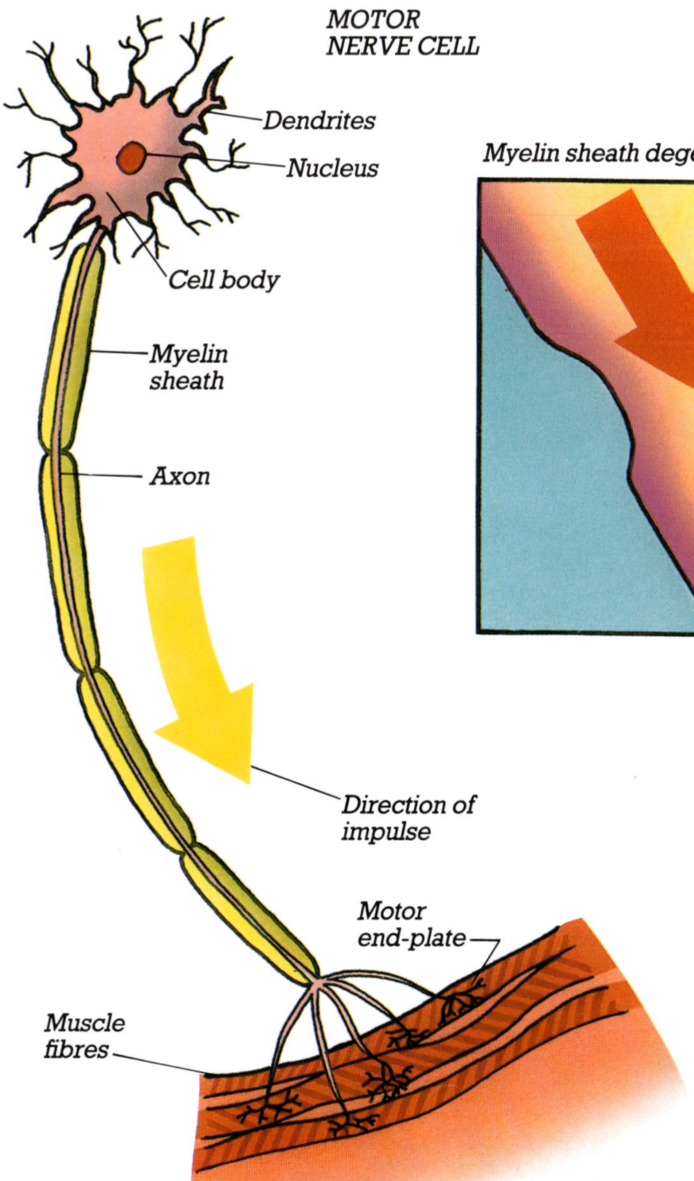

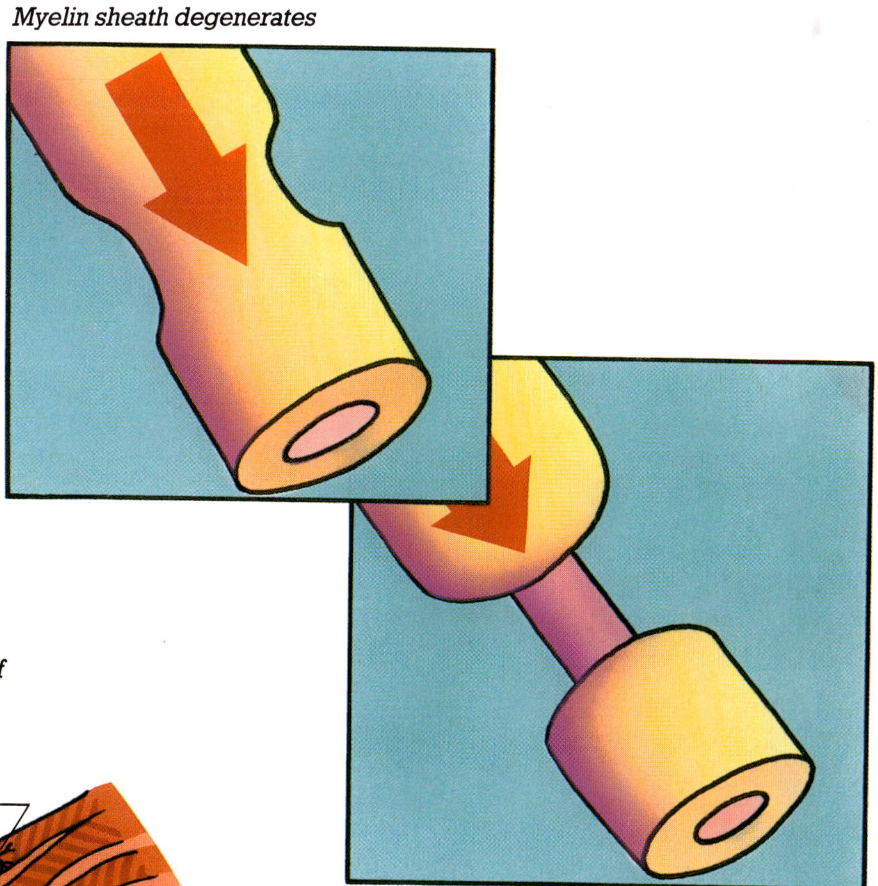

When the axon is exposed, the signal does not get through.

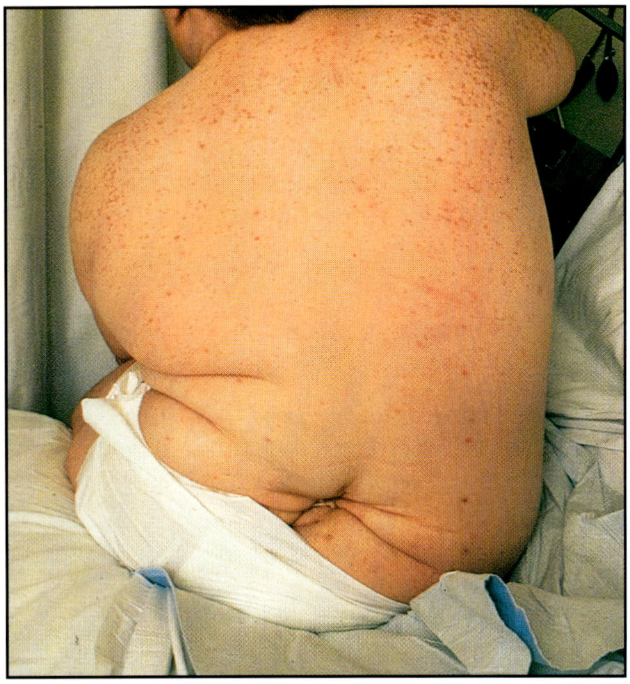

Spina bifida

Spina bifida

Spina bifida is a condition in which the spine and spinal cord are malformed during foetal development. The disease develops in the embryo at a very early stage of its growth in the mother's womb.

The spinal column consists of bony vertebrae and a spinal cord, and starts as a flat strip of cells in the embryo. The two edges of this strip grow into ridges and then over to form a tube. The inner part becomes the spinal cord, the outer forms the bony vertebrae. In spina bifida the edges of either or both of these layers do not grow together properly. This defect is most common in the lower part of the back. It is often harmless and can only be detected by X-rays. However, in some cases there are serious problems involving the spinal cord and its nerves.

The normal spinal cord

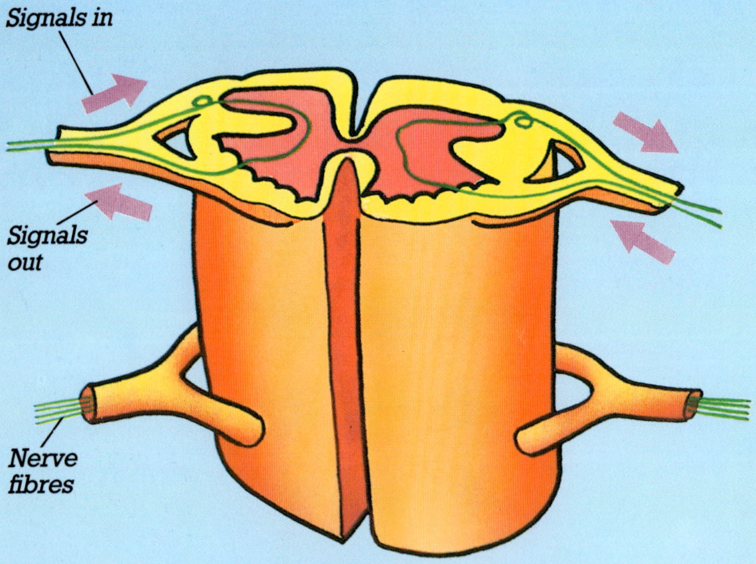

The spinal cord consists of an important highway of nerve cells and nerve fibres running through the narrow hollow of the backbone, from the brain to the lower part of the back. It contains some of the body's most complex and delicate cells. As the diagrams on this page show, it has a central area in the shape of an "H" surrounded by an oval. This "H" is mostly nerve cells. The oval consists of nerve fibres.

The spinal cord is surrounded by three protective membranes called meninges. The three layers are called the dura mater, arachnoid and pia mater. There is also cerebrospinal fluid between the meninges and the spinal cord. Pairs of nerve fibres branch out and leave the spinal cord between the vertebrae. These link the brain to all levels of the body. A great many of the body's simple movements and involuntary actions are coordinated by reflexes in the spinal cord.

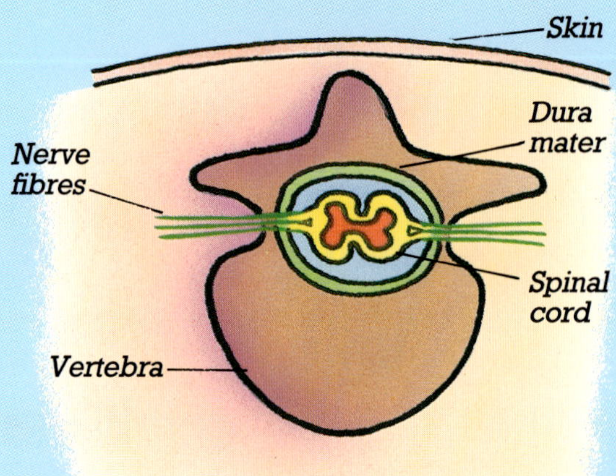

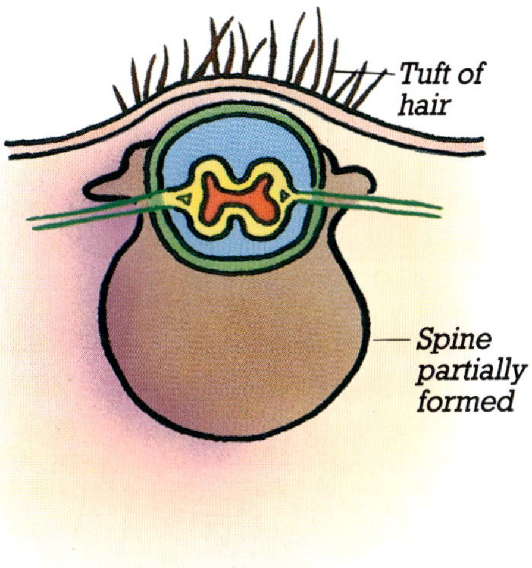

SPINA BIFIDA OCCULTA

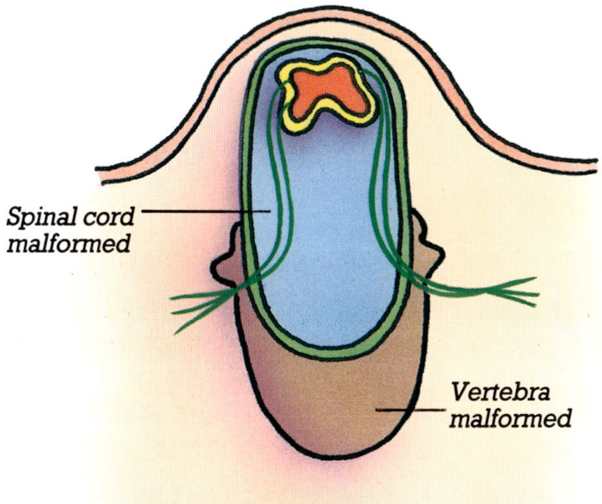

SPINA BIFIDA WITH MENINGOMYELOCOELE

What happens in spina bifida

There are varying degrees of deficiency in parts of the vertebral tube and spinal cord. If the soft tissues are normal or the deficiency is only in the bone, then it is called a spina bifida occulta. (See above left.) Its presence may be shown by a slight swelling or a tuft of hair. If the deficiency is wider, and has a bulging cyst of cerebrospinal fluid, it is a meningocoele.

Where the nerves or spinal cord are involved it is called a meningomyelocoele. (See above right.) The spinal cord and its coverings may be split wide open in a serious condition called spina bifida meyeloschisis. These two conditions can cause physical handicap, as the nerves and spinal cord may be damaged by being stretched and exposed.

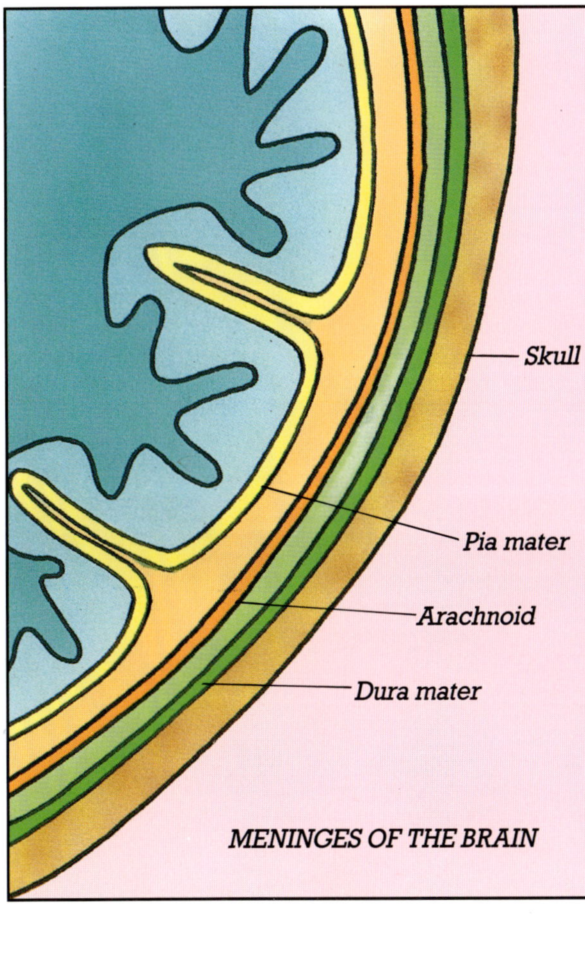

MENINGES OF THE BRAIN

Meningitis

Meningitis is an inflammation of the meninges, the membranes that cover and protect the central nervous system in the brain and spinal cord. There are a number of possible causes, including bacteria, viral and fungal infections. The most common with children is meningococcus, which can enter the body through the nose and spread to the brain via the bloodstream. Symptoms include vomiting, a high fever and severe headache. Often the disease is successfully treated, but sometimes not before it has damaged the brain. Scar tissue following the infection may prevent it from functioning properly. The result can be physical handicaps such as spasticity, deafness, mental defects, blindness, muscular contractures or even paralysis. Fortunately, there is a vaccine against meningococcus which can be used to control outbreaks of the disease.

Poliomyelitis

This is a disease which mainly affects children. It is an acute viral infection of the spinal cord that attacks the nerves which control the muscles. Severe cases of "polio", as it is often called, can end in paralysis or death. There are many people alive today who are disabled due to this disease. In the past 35 years a vaccine has been available which protects children from polio.

The virus enters the body through the mouth, throat or gut. It usually comes from poor sanitation, infected drinking water, or even bathing beaches which have been contaminated with sewage. Many people catch polio and only suffer from mild flu-like symptoms. But in its paralytic form this disease has killed 15 out of every 100 people infected. Children are most susceptible to this disease, but can be protected by vaccination.

The diagram below shows a section of the spinal cord damaged by poliomyelitis. The "H" of motor nerve cells which control the muscles has been partially destroyed, causing paralysis. When paralysis occurs affected limbs have to be positioned and exercised to prevent them going rigid. During convalescence, massage and a regime of exercises carefully worked out by a physiotherapist are needed to help regain limb movement and prevent further problems due to muscular imbalance.

Polio is still common in some countries where standards of hygiene and health care are very low. Over half the people in the Third World have no safe drinking water and three-quarters have no form of sewage control at all. A great many of them live in overcrowded slums, where the effects of poor sanitation are greatly multiplied. Unfortunately, many governments cannot afford to pay for a programme of vaccinations which would cut down the risks of catching the disease.

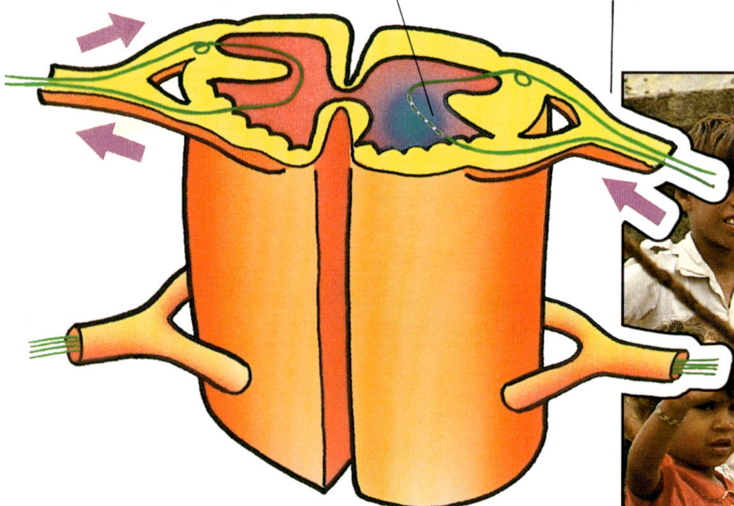

The diagram above shows a section of the spinal cord damaged by the poliomyelitis virus

Children who live in poverty-stricken countries are quite likely to catch polio from water polluted with sewage. If they become physically disabled, there is often little help on offer to them.

The neuromuscular system

Nerves and muscles work together to make the body move. The diagram on the right shows the intricate path that a nerve impulse follows. Once our minds decide how and when to move, nerve impulses speed from the cerebrum, or fore-brain, to the medulla, or hind-brain, where they switch sides and enter the spinal cord. Here they move to the front of the "H" of motor cells. Then they pass through to the motor nerve, and out into the muscle. On arrival the nerve impulse splits and passes into many tiny branches, each one entering a muscle fibre. Each muscle fibre contains tiny fibrils or rods which are stimulated by the nerve impulse to contract or relax the muscle concerned and thus create movement.

There is also a sensory role in every movement. There are sensory endings in the nerves themselves, in the tendons, ligaments and connective tissues associated with them. However, much work is done by the spinal reflexes. They coordinate the opposite sides of the body. For example, if you lift one leg while standing, the reflexes work to contract the muscles in the other leg to support the added weight.

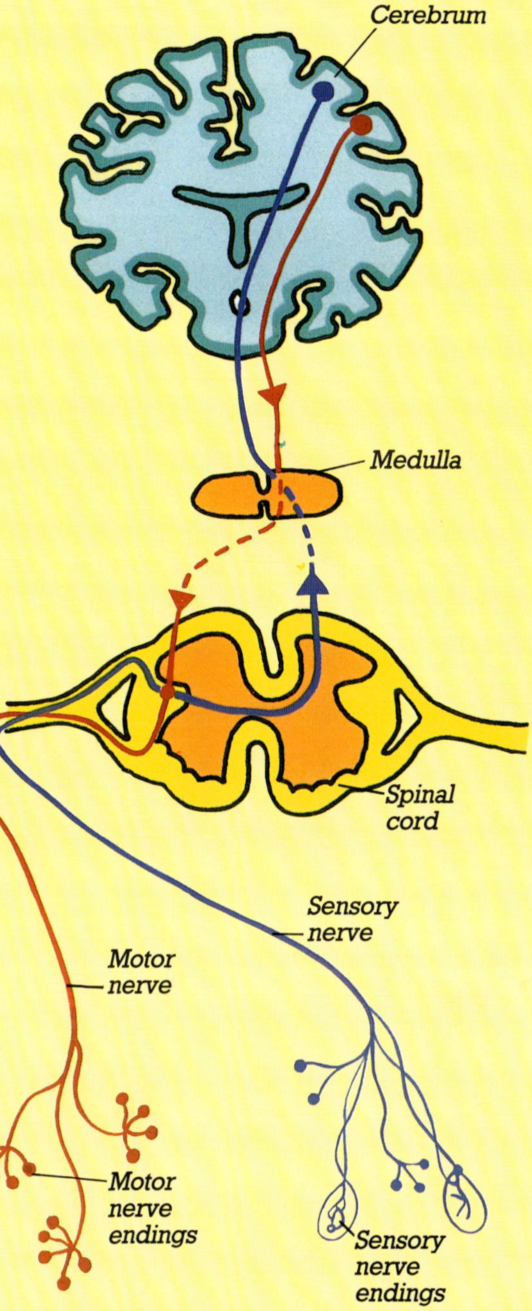

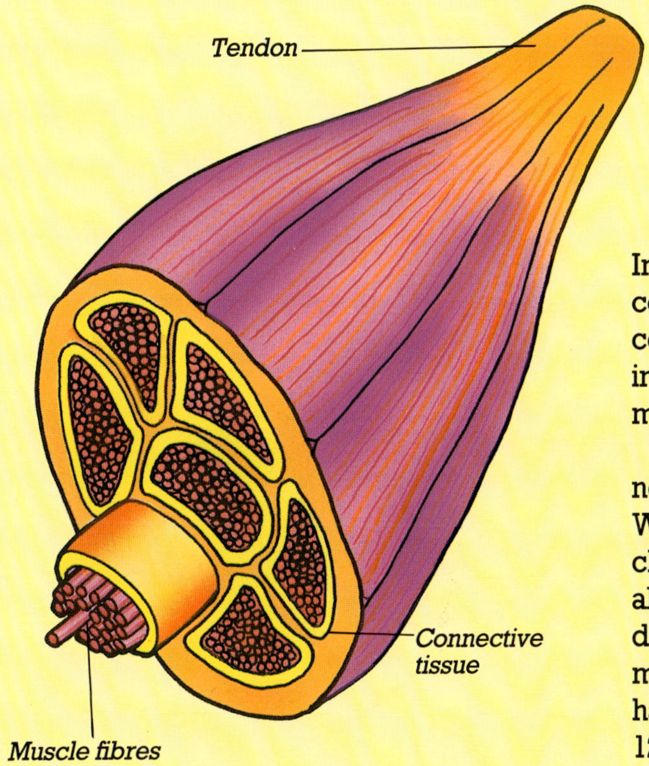

Impulses also pass up to and down from the cerebellum to effect a smooth movement. The cerebellum is the part of the brain particularly involved in coordination of complex muscular movements.

The control and coordination of the whole neuromuscular system is extremely complex. We can only marvel at the way the body changes a wish into a smooth movement. Its ability outstrips any computer. It follows that damage to any part of such a complex system may result in a serious disability. This is what happens in muscular dystrophy. (See page 12).

Muscular dystrophy

Muscular dystrophy is the name given to a group of muscle disorders which have many symptoms in common. They result from errors in the development of muscle fibres. All the different types of muscular dystrophy are inherited. Sometimes they only affect one sex, sometimes both, depending on the kind of muscular dystrophy. The disorder gradually leads to weakness and wasting of the muscles.

Impressive names have been given to each kind of muscular dystrophy, depending on which groups of muscles they affect and who first described the condition. Muscular dystrophy can develop any time from early childhood to adulthood. Often several members of the same family suffer from it. The nerves serving the muscles are not affected. The diagram below shows the Duchenne type of muscular dystrophy. In this case the muscle fibres are destroyed and become larger because of the excessive deposits of fat and connective tissue.

Both sides of the body can be equally affected by muscular dystrophy. A waddling gait and difficulty getting up from a chair are usual early indications of its presence. The muscular weakness gets progressively worse. Sufferers find that they can no longer get up or walk. Later they find it difficult to dress themselves and perform other personal tasks. There may be a gradual deterioration over many years. There is no certain cure, but physiotherapy and orthopaedic techniques help to counteract deformities and muscular contractures. The families involved need to think seriously about having more children since there are risks that the disease will occur in future generations.

Although the outlook is not good for sufferers of some types of this disease, much can be done to help them live with the physical handicap. Children who have muscular dystrophy are often cheerful and bright with a very good learning capacity. There are many cases of sufferers who lead happy, fulfilled lives.

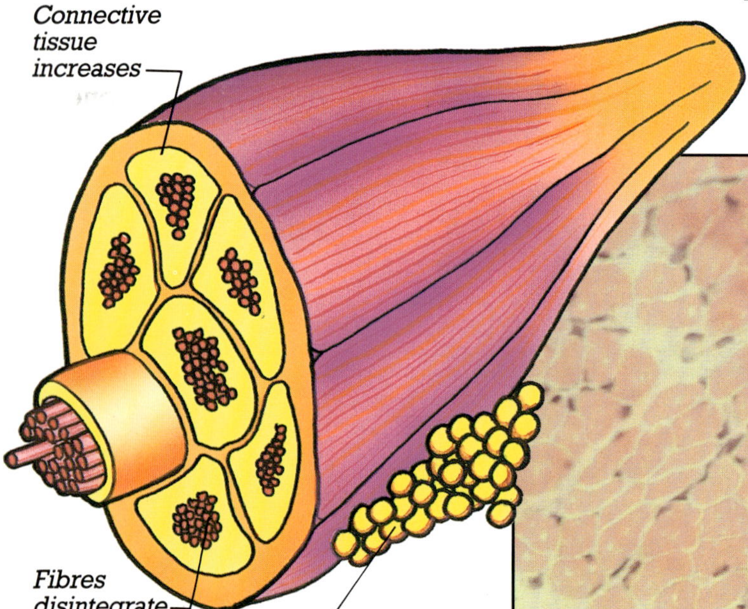

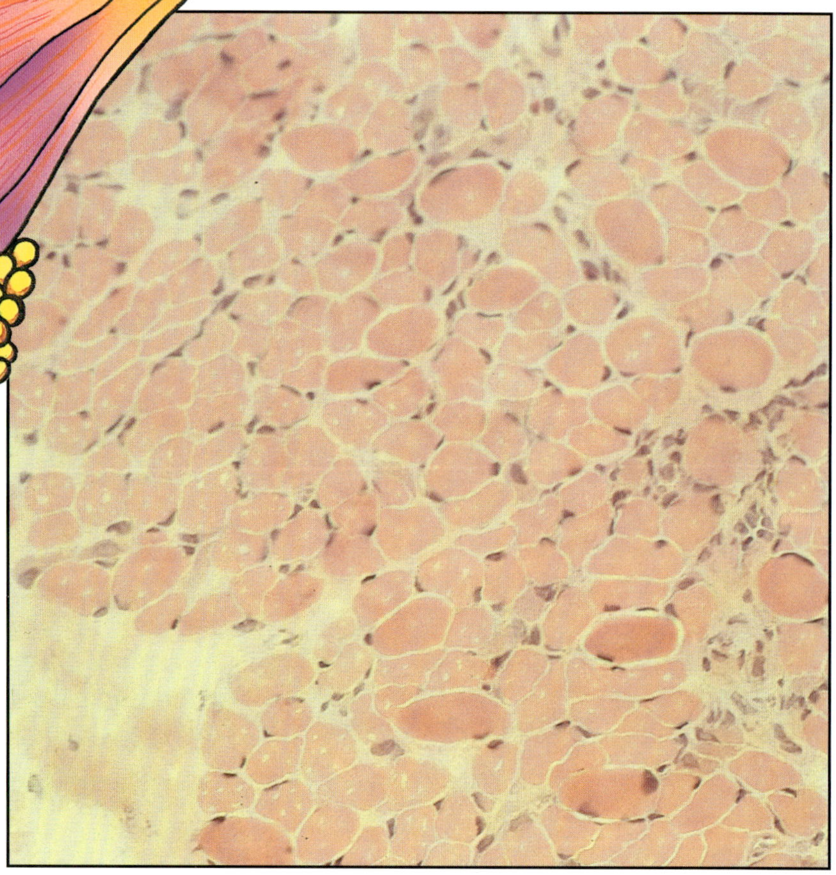

Excessive deposits of fat in the muscles in the Duchenne type of muscular dystrophy

THROMBOSIS

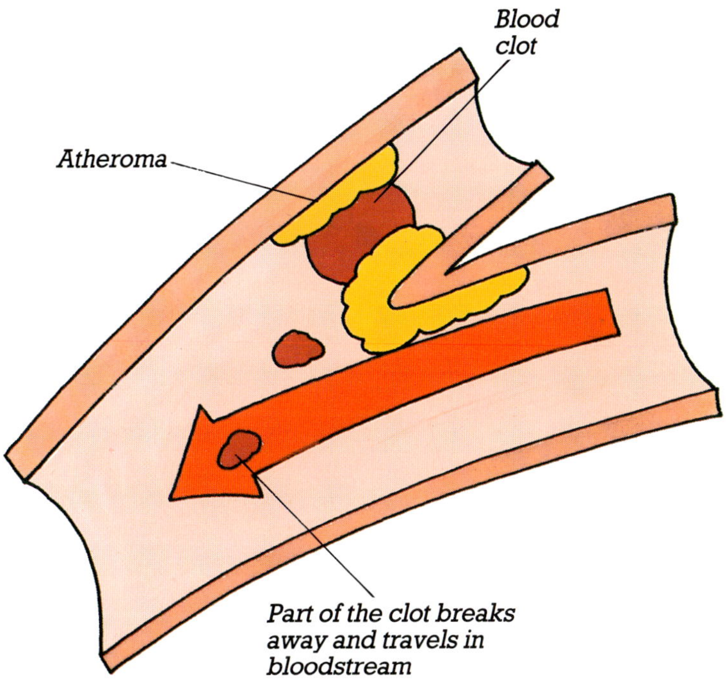

Damage in left-hand side of the brain from clot (thrombosis) or burst vessel (aneurysm)

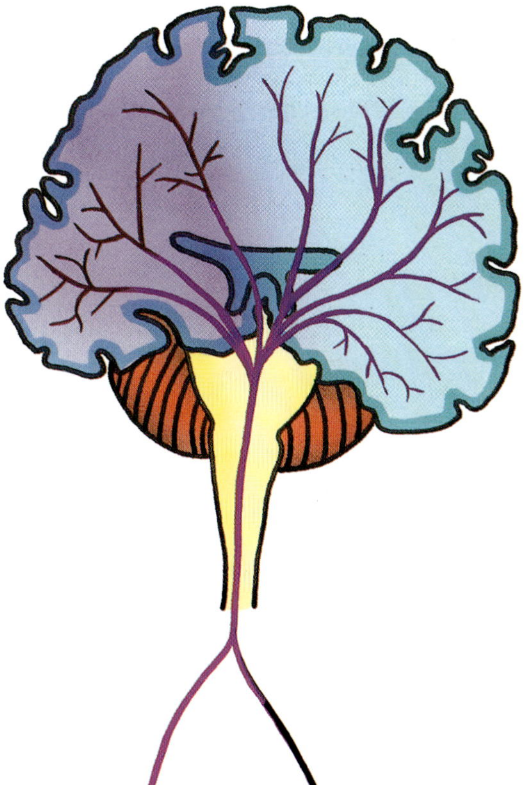

Damage in left-hand side of the brain affects right-hand side of body

Stroke

A stroke is a sudden loss of muscular control or sensory ability due to lesion (a wound, sore or tumour) in the brain. The commonest cause is damage to the blood supply because blood carries oxygen from the lungs to the brain. Brain tissue will cease to function if its oxygen supply is cut off.

Blood is pumped through the entire body by the heart through blood vessels. Inevitably, the system wears out over the years. In old age, clots of blood can form in the heart and blood vessels. This is known as a thrombosis. Clots can break up and travel to the brain. If any of these block a blood vessel a stroke will result. Another reason for strokes is that arteries in the body clog up over the years. A substance called atheroma is deposited and clots form on it. (See diagram top left).

Sometimes the walls of the body's blood vessels become thinned. They can then swell, forming an aneurysm. (See diagram below). If they burst the result is damage to the nerve tissue and a loss of body function. In some cases the brain can no longer tell the muscles what to do. Because of the way the nervous system works, the damage is confined to one side of the body. If the damage is not too severe, it will heal itself with time and some function will return. Physiotherapy is very important in the weeks following a stroke and can speed recovery.

ANEURYSM

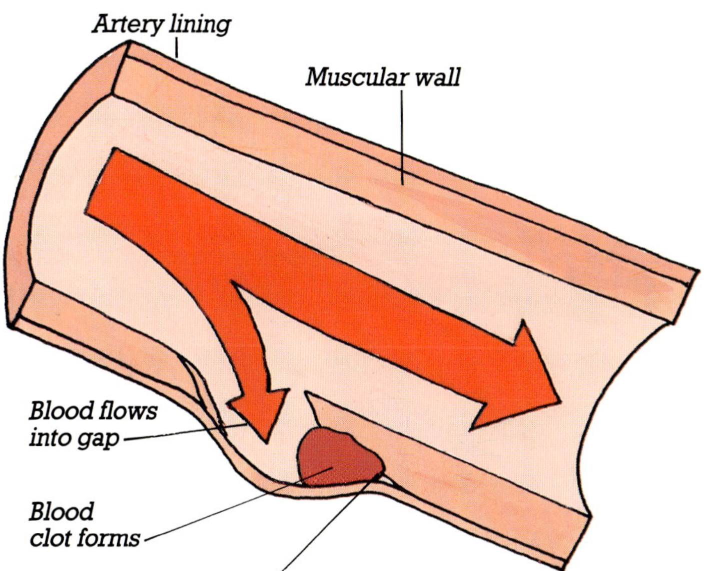

Joints and bones

A great many cases of physical handicap are caused by problems with bones and joints. Osteoarthritis is by far the most common cause of chronic disability, but this disease seldom occurs before the age of 50 except where there has been damage to the joint. The main weight-bearing joints in the body, i.e. the spine, knees or hips, are the ones which tend to be most often attacked. The cartilage lining of the joint surface, which protects the underlying bone, can be damaged by an accident, over-use or old age. The underlying bone is exposed or becomes deformed and inflammation results. Irregular bone growth follows. There is scarring around the joint and movement becomes more difficult.

In rheumatoid arthritis the joints at the ends of the body, such as those of the fingers, toes, wrists and ankles, are affected. They become stiff, swollen and deformed. The cause is unknown, and treatment is usually restricted to pain-killing drugs.

Osteoporosis, "brittle bones", is very common in women over 50 years of age. There is a loss of bony substance which contributes to loss of height, increased stoop, hip fractures and rib cage movements. There is a tendency for bones to fracture easily. Osteomalacia, or "rickets", causes a softening and sometimes bending of the bones. This is usually caused by a lack of vitamin D and too little exposure to sunlight.

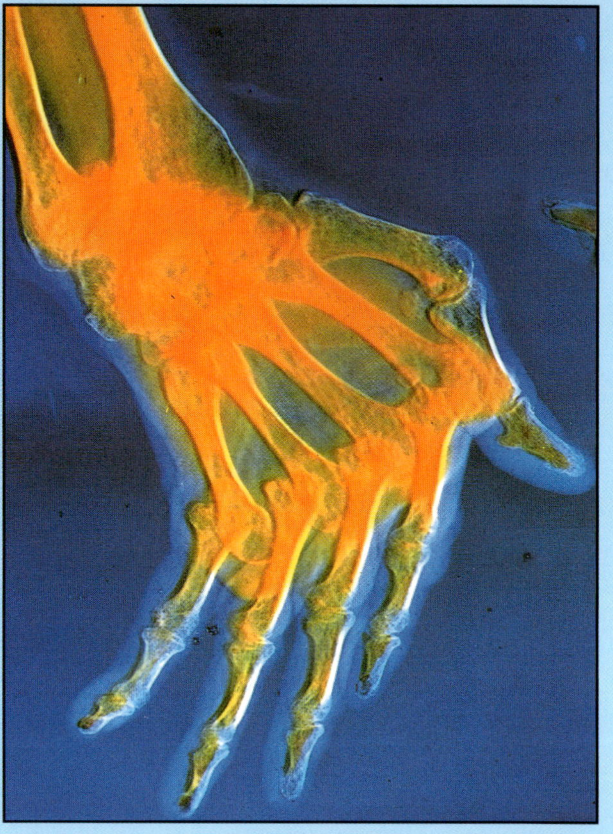

An X-ray showing damage to the joints of the hand caused by extreme rheumatoid arthritis

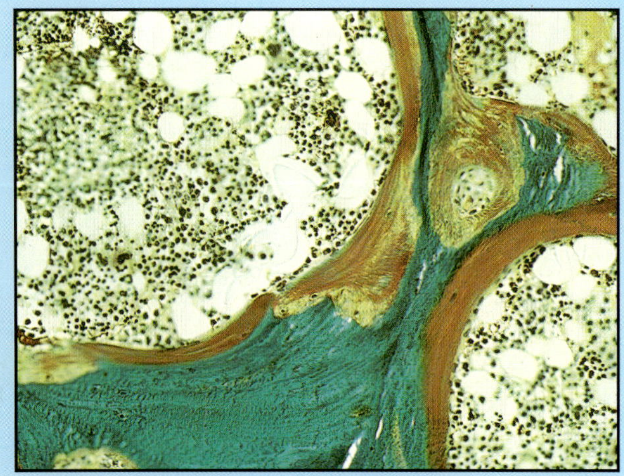

A micro-photograph of osteomalacia. The brown areas show where the bones have softened.

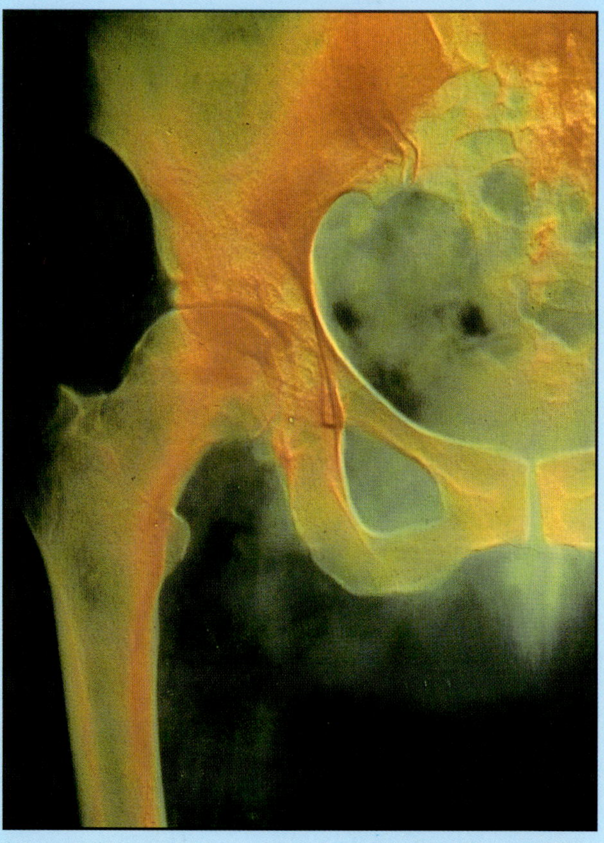

An X-ray showing damage to a hip joint caused by osteoarthritis

Disorders of the senses

Blindness and deafness are major handicaps because we use vision and hearing more than any other senses. There are three main causes of blindness in Great Britain. They are glaucoma, cataracts and senile degeneration of the retina at the back of the eye.

Glaucoma is blindness caused by an increase in pressure of the fluid in the eye. Fluid is constantly being made within an eye. It normally drains through a tiny tube into veins on the surface of the eyeball. In glaucoma this tube becomes blocked and pressure in the eye rises. This damages the delicate nerves and light receptors at the back of the eye. Blindness results if it is left untreated. Cataract is a cloudiness of the lens of the eye. It is associated with old age. It is also common in diabetics. There is increasing mistiness of the vision until blindness results. Senile, or macular, degeneration of the retina is a gradual dying off of the light receptors at the back of the eye. They transmit light images to the optic nerve, which passes them on to the part of the brain which receives vision. It is a part of old age. Nothing can be done to halt its progress, which fortunately is very slow.

Deafness is a handicap that children can be born with. However, it may be some time before it is identified by a doctor. Once detected the child can be taught how to communicate. The problem is very different if the person has been able to hear and then loses the sense of hearing, since the brain will have already learned speech patterns. The muscles of speech in the larynx, throat, tongue and lips have already been taught how to work. But even when the ear and hearing nerves to the brain are severely damaged, children will always benefit from learning aids and special training.

Acquired deafness is caused by middle ear infections following colds, and inner ear disease resulting from measles, mumps and influenza. Meningitis can damage the parts of the brain associated with hearing or the auditory nerve that passes into the brain from the ear. Deafness may be due to a blockage in the tubes between the back of the nose and ears. It can even be caused by wax in the outer ear passage which can be syringed clean. If all else fails there are very effective hearing aids available nowadays that are highly sensitive in spite of being very small.

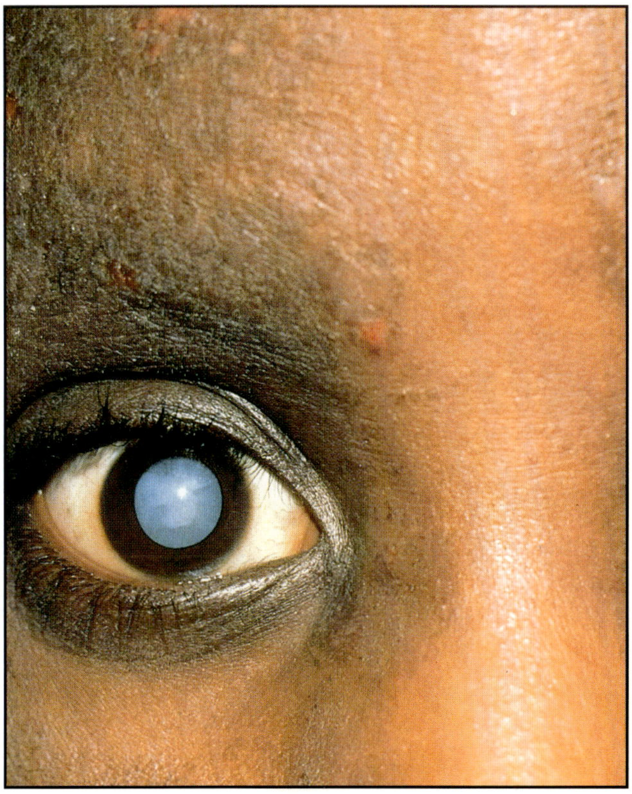

Blindness caused by a cataract

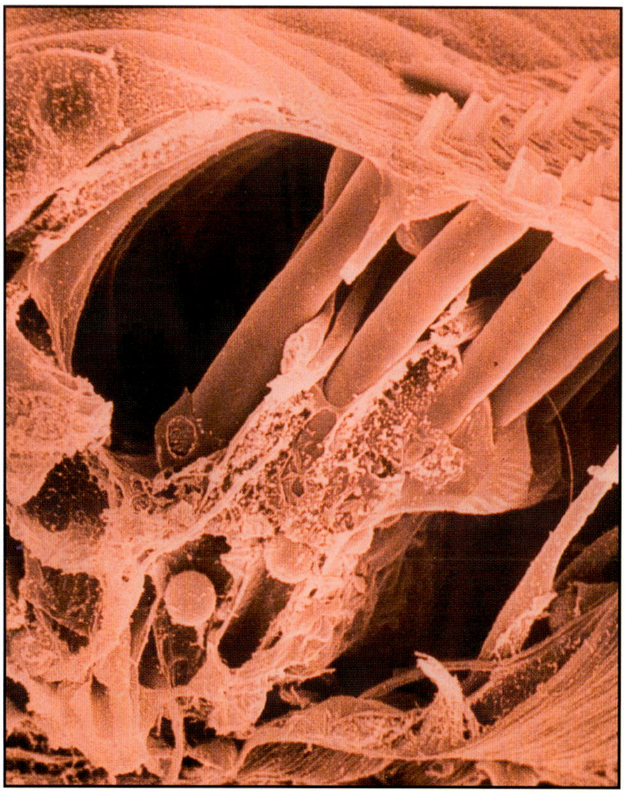

The inner ear, where auditory nerve deafness can occur

Cerebral palsy and congenital disorders

Children can be born with, or acquire, a number of conditions which can result in physical handicap. These are known as congenital disorders. Cerebral palsy is a general term for various conditions that result from damage to the brain at or around the time of birth. It is a paralysis of one or more parts of the body caused by disorders of the brain. It is sometimes associated with types of mental retardation. Cerebral palsy creates spastic or stiff paralysis. A child with this disease may seem to be perfectly normal until he or she sits up and starts to move. Sometimes cerebral palsy is caused by difficulties at birth. If a baby lacks oxygen for many minutes it can lose essential brain cells which cannot be replaced. Skull fractures and associated brain haemorrhages can also cause cerebral palsy if they are not operated on.

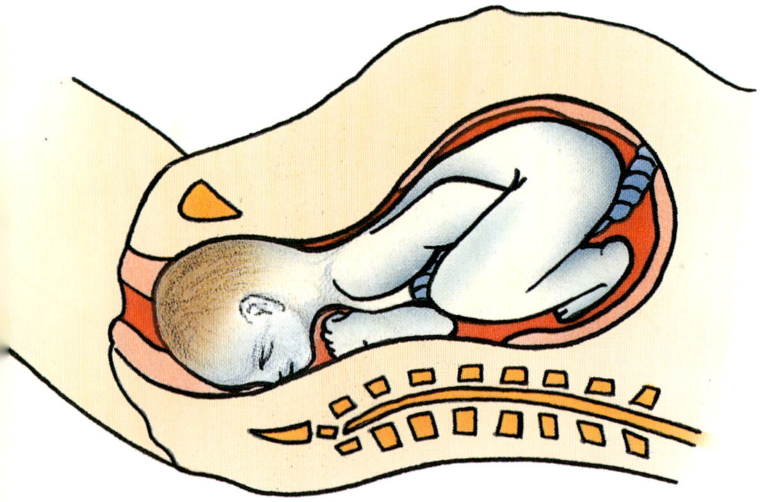

In a difficult birth, a baby may be deprived of oxygen.

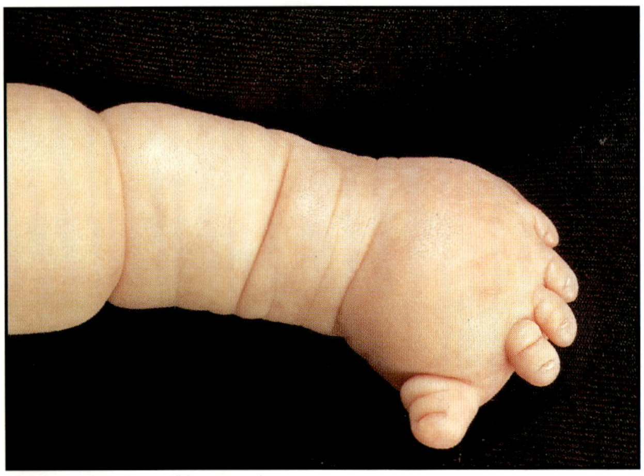

Congenital malformation

Congenital dislocation of the hip is another condition acquired early in life. The head of the femur (thigh bone) lies outside its cup (the acetabulum) on the pelvis. If left untreated it will cause a permanent limp. It is easily detected soon after birth and can be treated with the simplest of temporary splints.

Clubfoot is thought to be due to the way the baby lies in the womb before birth. The foot is rotated inwards. There is shortening of both the achilles tendon and the ligaments beneath the foot. It can be corrected by manipulation and splints. If this fails, an operation may achieve good results.

Thalidomide

Drugs can cause physical handicap. Twenty-five years ago babies were born without limbs (see photo below), following the use of thalidomide in pregnancy. The drug had been taken by mothers in order to relieve the feeling of sickness that frequently accompanies pregnancy. These days drugs have to undergo extensive testing to make sure they do not damage the unborn child. But it is always best for a pregnant woman to consult a doctor before taking any drugs.

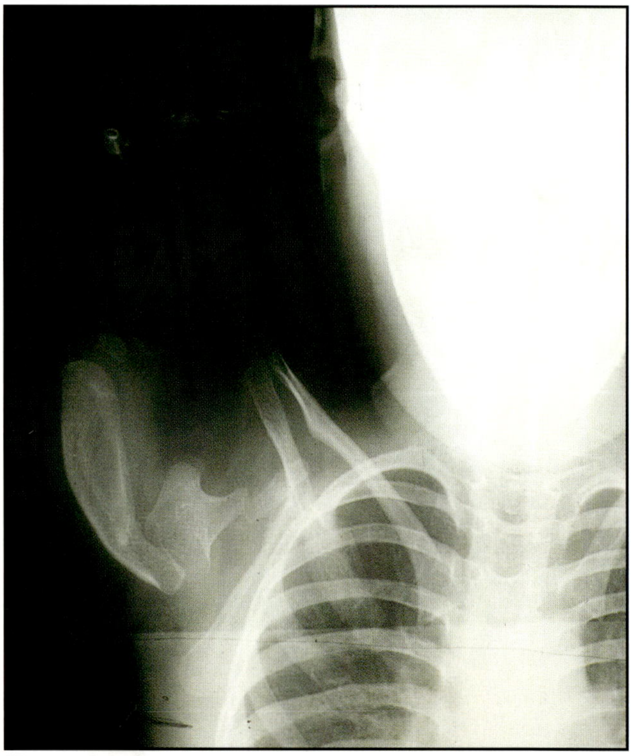

X-ray of thalidomide baby

Accidents

Accidents are the most common cause of death in childhood, and of physical handicap. Car crashes or accidents involving pedestrians or bicycles on the road are very frequent. It is very easy to damage the head in any of these types of accident, and this often affects the brain. A skull fracture may cause a piece of bone to become embedded in the brain. Depending on which part of the brain is damaged there will be a loss of body function. Loss of control of the limbs or loss of sensation could result. There also may be loss of memory, and even a personality change.

Spinal fractures are common in car crashes, but the real danger comes from damage to the spinal cord. This may cause paralysis below the part damaged. If the spinal cord in the neck is cut it will cause paralysis and loss of sensation in both arms and legs. If it is at chest level the function of the arms is preserved but there is loss of function in the legs and lack of bladder and bowel control. Injuries to the pelvis and legs can cause deformity. Loss of a limb would be a considerable disability. However, superb artificial limbs can now be fitted, making many jobs possible. Douglas Bader (later knighted for his outstanding record of bravery) was a celebrated fighter pilot in the Second World War. He had two artificial legs.

Young children at play need to be supervised.

Sharp tools and machinery can be dangerous.

Thousands of people are injured, or killed, in road accidents every year.

TREATMENT OF DISABILITIES

In the world we live in it is impossible to prevent all disabilities. The next best solution is to detect them as early as possible so that they may be treated and perhaps prevented from developing into a permanent problem. When damage is done, then the greatest care has to be taken to try to restore or repair the affected parts. Where this is not possible, use of artificial aids, extra training and physiotherapy will help.

There may have to be changes in one's surroundings. A new type of home, transport or school may be necessary. Access ramps may have to be built, or special aids may have to be worn. People may need counselling, and the encouragement, support and companionship of other people. Above all a doctor or social worker will need to explain the nature of the illness in order to help the affected persons live with it. It is always better to know what is going to happen rather than live with uncertainty.

Drugs

Drugs are a great help in treating and preventing disability. Meningitis is one of the most feared infections. It can be caused by several different organisms. Each of these is dealt with by a different drug. It is important to remove a little of the cerebro- spinal fluid which surrounds the brain and spinal cord so that it can be examined to identify the particular infection. Some antibiotics are injected directly into the cerebrospinal fluid through a needle inserted into the spine. However, usually they can be given as medicine by mouth. Antibiotics are also used to treat severe middle ear infections to prevent deafness.

Many disabilities are the result of arthritis. The effects of the two main types, osteo-arthritis and rheumatoid arthritis, can be lessened by drugs which diminish the inflammation in the affected joints. Such drugs are ibuprofen, naproxen, indonethacid and steroids. Injection of gold salts is also very useful. Aspirin is a drug widely used to treat and prevent disability, and has been used in the treatment of arthritis. Like the other drugs it reduces the inflammatory process in the joints. Scurvy and rickets once were a common cause of arthritis. They can be prevented by vitamins. Extra calcium may be useful in helping to prevent osteoporosis.

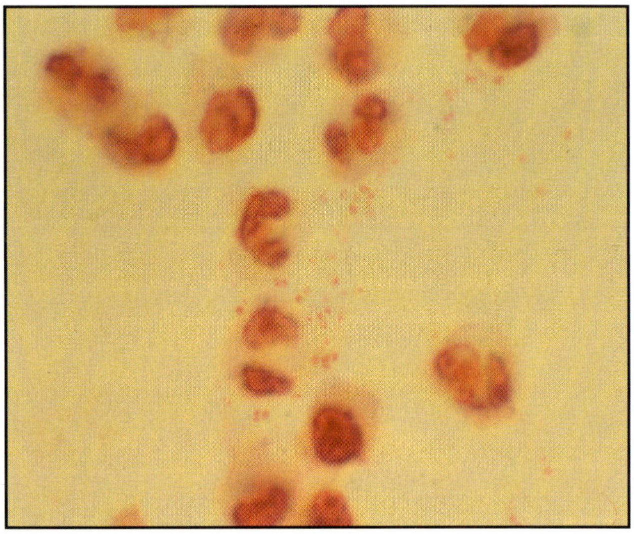

Examination of cerebrospinal fluid reveals meningitis.

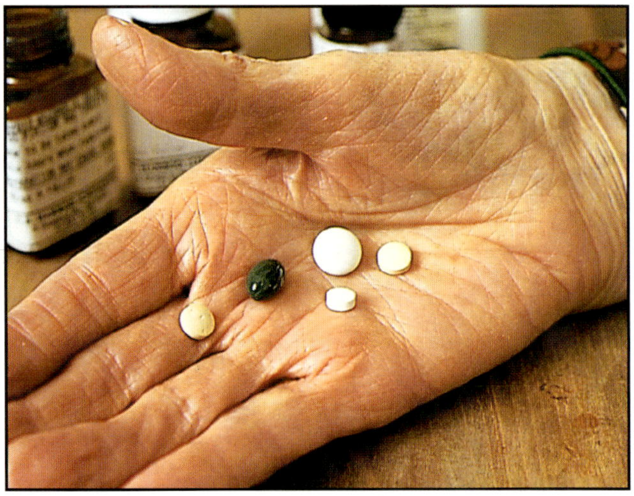

Although many handicaps cannot be cured, relief may be given with drugs.

Before birth

A mother-to-be may have a number of routine tests during pregnancy. These may detect or prevent many physical handicaps in her unborn child. Ultrasound in early pregnancy will find any serious abnormalities. The technique is like the old method of detecting submarines, by pinging sounds through water and measuring their echoes. A medical instrument is drawn back and forth across the mother's abdomen, and the echoes form an image of the baby on a screen.

Routine examinations during pregnancy will detect any rise in the mother's blood pressure. Such a rise can lead to premature labour and the birth of a baby not yet completely formed. If a baby is born too early it is prone to mental deficiency and cerebral palsy.

In early pregnancy mothers-to-be are tested for syphylis. This infection used to be a potent cause of handicap. It is now rare. At the same time she is rhesus blood grouped. This is to detect or prevent antibodies being formed by the mother against the child's blood.

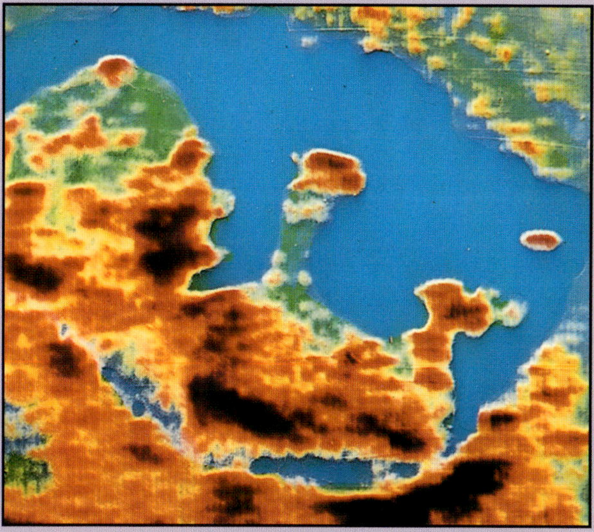
An ultrasound image of a baby in the womb will show if all the limbs are present.

Other blood tests in pregnancy are useful in preventing physical handicap. Anaemia is a lowered haemoglobin level in the blood. Haemoglobin carries oxygen to the foetus. If the level is low during birth, oxygen starvation of the baby's brain can result. In spina bifida a specific protein is released and finds its way into the mother's bloodstream. If this is detected, a foetoscope, which is a fibre-optic inspecting torch, is introduced into the womb and the foetus is carefully examined.

The amniotic fluid and foetal blood can be tested for other conditions known to cause physical handicap. The incidence of Down's Syndrome children increases after the mother reaches 35. Amniotic fluid or foetal blood can be examined for other genetic abnormalities. The likelihood of certain types of muscular dystrophy can be shown, as can nearly 40 other kinds of abnormalities.

Nowadays children are given a combined mumps, measles and rubella vaccine. The rubella part will prevent German measles being caught. While not necessarily a serious illness itself, if it is caught by a pregnant woman it can cause severe physical deformity in her baby.

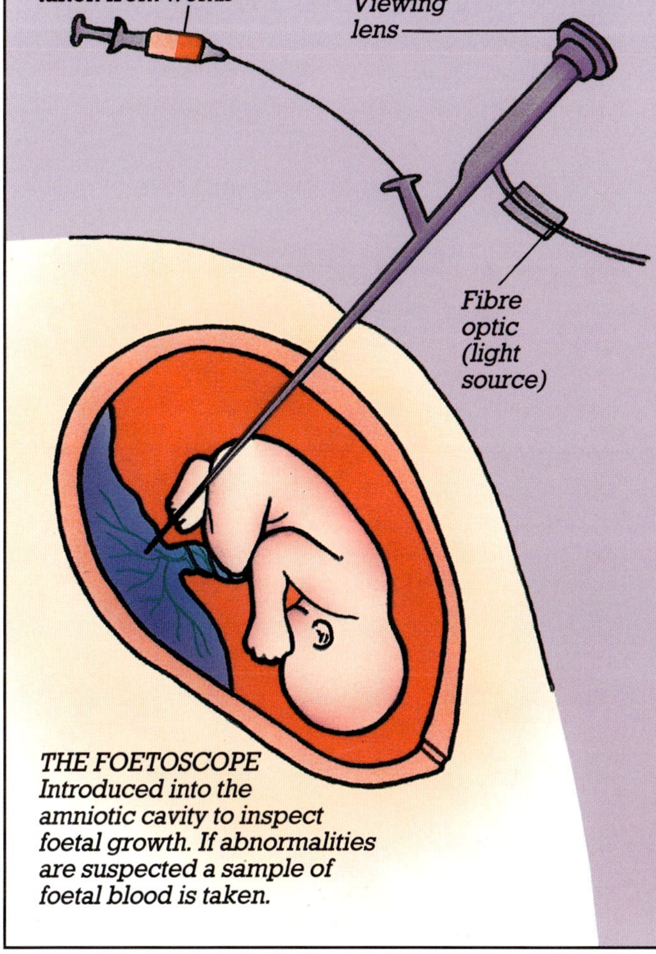

THE FOETOSCOPE Introduced into the amniotic cavity to inspect foetal growth. If abnormalities are suspected a sample of foetal blood is taken.

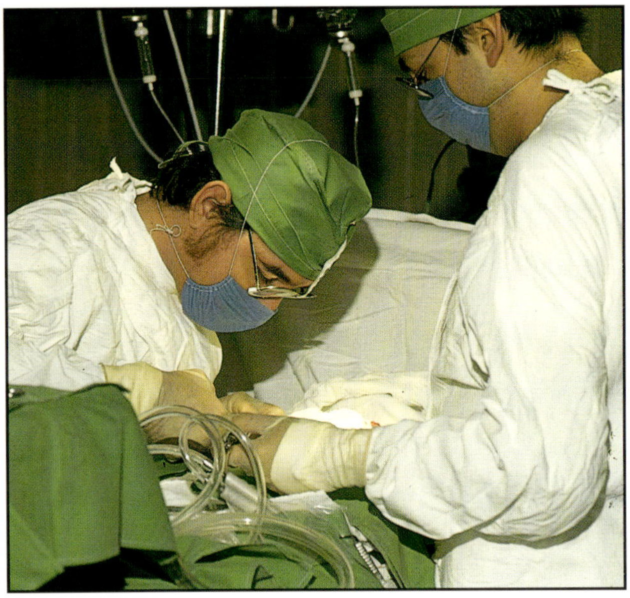

In some cases surgery helps.

Surgery

The surgeon can have a large part to play in the prevention and treatment of physical handicap. There are so many ways in which a skilled surgeon can help the physically handicapped that only the briefest mention can be made of some of the possible operations. Most have been developed only in the last 50 years. Some spina bifida defects can be removed or repaired. An aneurysm or a blood vessel in the brain can be repaired even if there has been a stroke. There are hip and knee replacements possible for severe cases of arthritis. Eye cataracts can be removed and pressure caused by glaucoma can be lowered. Clubfoot can also be corrected.

Specialist retraining

Sometimes an aneurysm or blood vessel bursts at the base of the brain and causes a stroke. The person is often left with partial paralysis of one half of the body. Specialist physiotherapy and retraining are needed. Passive movements (those done by the therapist for the patient) of the affected limbs are begun soon afterwards to prevent stiffening up of the muscles. When there has been sufficient recovery, the physiotherapist encourages the patient to perform active movements (those done by the patient) against gradually increasing resistance. As power returns to the limbs increasingly skilled movements are encouraged. The patient is shown how to use both arms and legs in every movement, whether sitting, walking or lying down. In this way coordination of different groups of muscles is maintained. A good physiotherapist gives the patient the confidence and enthusiasm to get better. Much depends on the patient's own desire and determination to improve.

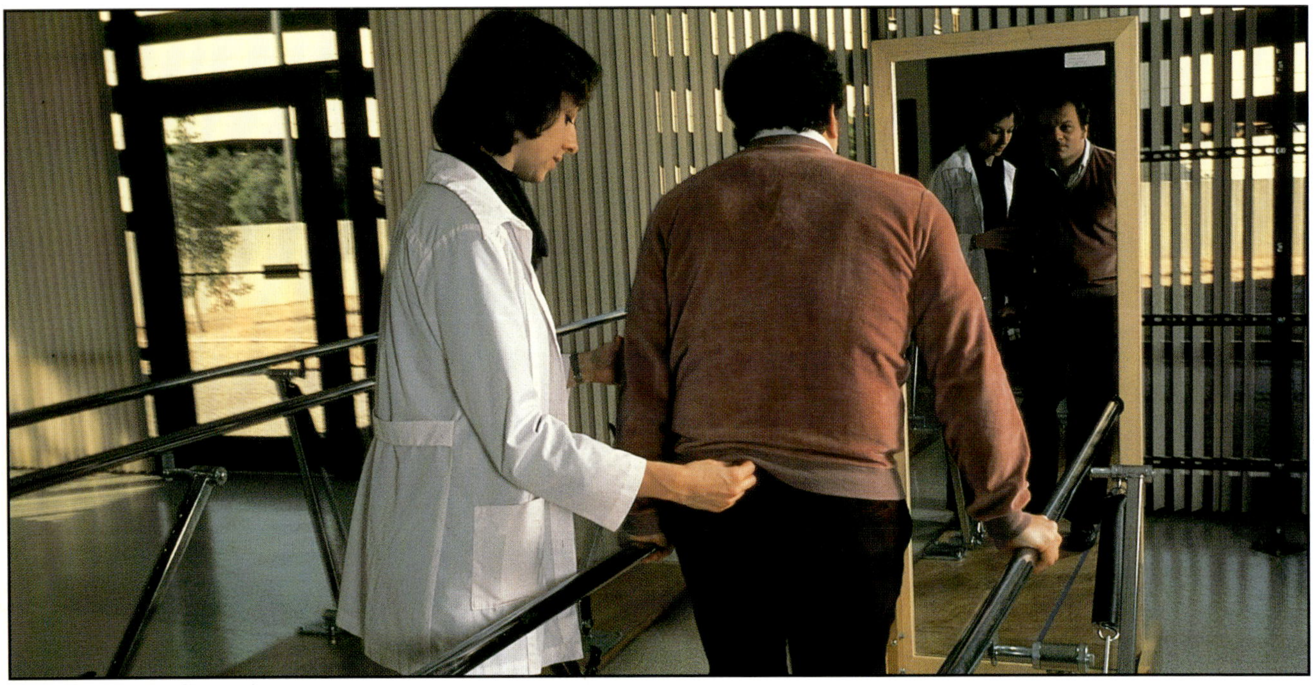

Learning to walk again

A handicapped boy getting exercise and learning coordination with the help of a physiotherapist

Physiotherapy

Physiotherapy is a very important help to the physically handicapped. It cuts down the possible damage and makes use of whatever abilities are left. It helps to mobilise joints, strengthen muscles and improve coordination and balance. Joints are moved as fully as possible, without inflicting pain, through gentle pressure from the physiotherapist's hand. In muscle strengthening exercises, muscles are encouraged to contract against resistance. Weights and springs are used to oppose the muscles. Coordination is often taught by practising movements such as lifting an arm or leg, sitting down, walking or putting on clothes.

Passive movements preserve full mobility. They stop the muscle from permanent shortening. They help to maintain the muscles while, as in poliomyelitis, the diseased nerve cells which control them can recover. Muscles can also be maintained by electric shocks to the nerves that supply them.

Braces

Splints and braces have their place in helping the physically handicapped. In cerebral palsy they are useful in overcoming deformities caused by spastic muscles. The deformity is corrected by gradually stretching the contracted muscles, which are then held in place for three months. After that, removable braces or splints are used indefinitely to prevent recurrence of the deformity . External support by a brace or caliper to the ankle or knee may help a stroke sufferer to walk when other methods have failed. A carefully applied "figure of 8" sling around both shoulders will help the painful shoulder of a paralysed arm. The same applies to polio sufferers. In this disease the muscles around the spine are more likely to be affected. A brace can be used to support it. The physical disabilities in rheumatoid arthritis are helped by lightweight splints. They help to immobilise the joints affected during an acute recurrence of the disease. A splint may also be helpful as a permanent support. A splinted knee may make all the difference between being chairbound and able to walk.

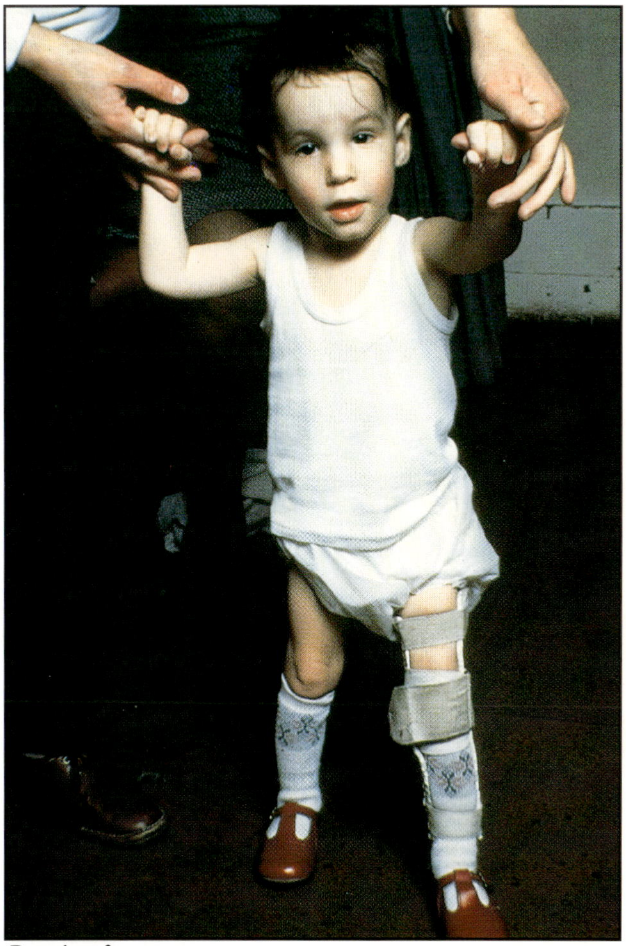

Bracing for support

LIVING WITH PHYSICAL HANDICAP

Nurses, doctors, physiotherapists and occupational therapists will have worked hard to improve the disability and achieve as much function as possible. Now the individual has to learn to cope with life. There may have to be adjustments to their homes. The toilet, bath and stairs may have to be adapted. Aids may be required for dressing, working, walking, eating and performing the many tasks which are part of everyday life. A home help might be necessary. Specially adapted transport may be needed to go shopping or get to work. Electric wheelchairs and small cars are available. Some travel firms arrange special holidays for the physically handicapped. More public transport is being adapted, with thought being given to the needs of the handicapped.

Special devices are available for hobbies such as gardening and sports. There are even paraplegic Olympics for those who want to take on the real challenge of competition.

Rehabilitation centres

There are rehabilitation centres for those determined to help themselves. Severely disabled young people can attend full-time residential centres. For the less severely disabled, who, for example, may have suffered a mild stroke, there are day units available. They can go home or back to hospital in the evening. They may need a programme of intensive rehabilitation with a good deal of physiotherapy and occupational therapy. Some industries have established their own rehabilitation units with special workshops to encourage their disabled employees to adjust more rapidly. In Britain the Manpower Services Commission has special responsibility for those who are handicapped by injury or chronic disease. Part of this is the Employment Services Division. The chronically disabled can register with them. They can get help with transport to and from work as well as any special equipment they might need.

A modern rehabilitation centre

You can never be too young or old to seek help with a physical handicap at a rehabilitation centre. Parents and children can have fun there. Both adults and children can meet those who will become friends and companions.

Artificial aids

There are many advanced aids available for physically handicapped people. Hearing aids are very small and reliable. New and improved models are constantly coming on to the market.

No one needs to remain limbless in this day and age. Artificial limbs can be specially made and new ones fitted as a person grows. There are even experimental computerised arms which pick up nerve impulses from the arm stump and translate them into moving hands and fingers.

Special computer keyboards are made with large keys, so that disabled people can use their hands instead of fingers. Some cerebral palsied children cannot talk but most people who suffer from this disease are bright and have a strong memory. It is possible for them to have a keyboard where figures represent words. By pressing the figures they can make up sentences. If necessary, a voice synthesizer can speak for them.

Those who cannot write can type out their school work on a computer and word processor. Drawing can now be done with a computer, as can geometry and design. Today's new technology can provide the means to overcome many of the obstacles a physical handicap can present.

There may be some great difficulties to be overcome when an artificial aid is first used. But once these are mastered, a new sense of achievement and freedom can become the rewards for all the effort.

A blind student using a print-to-voice machine

A deaf girl enjoys music with the help of a hearing aid.

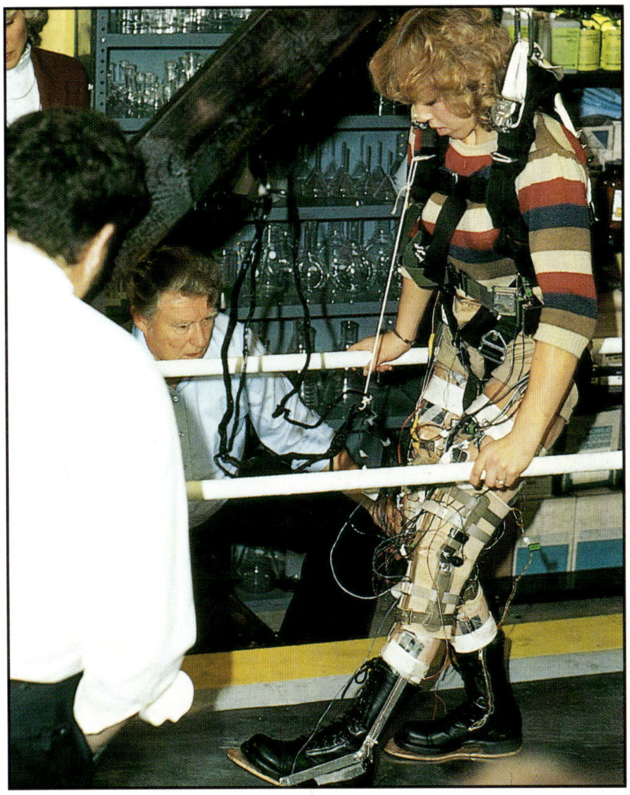

Walking with a harness and computer-driven aids

There is a reading system for the blind called Braille, which was invented in 1829 by Louis Braille. It is widely used in many countries. Raised dots represent letters, numbers and simple sounds. You may see it on bottles of linseed oil, surgical spirit and bleach in your local shops. It says, "Do not drink". There are even more advanced systems being developed for the blind (see photo left).

Help in the home

Help may be needed with washing, dressing, cooking, tidying-up and getting up and down stairs. Advice about bath aids can be obtained from occupational therapists and social services. There are many bath fitments for the handicapped. They range from soap made on a loop of cord, so that it doesn't get lost in the bathwater, to electric hoists. The bath itself may be modified with a non-slip rubber mat on the bottom. A board can be fitted across the top of the bath for sitting on. A heavy duty rail can be fitted to the wall beside the bath and toilet.

Dressing is often difficult for the disabled because fine motor movements are needed. Loose garments which do up at the front with simple fittings are helpful. Velcro is a very useful substitute for buttons or press studs on clothing. Long-handled tongs help to get socks on. Slip-on shoes avoid the problems of tying laces, but there are also elastic shoelaces and self-locking devices which hold the laces tight.

For independence while feeding, there is a combined knife, fork and spoon, and a special fork which can be clamped to the side of the plate which holds the food while it is cut up. Kitchens can be modified with special appliances and fitments to help prepare food.

For difficulties with moving up and down stairs there are specially designed platforms which can carry a disabled person. These are much less expensive than a vertical lift.

Strong rails provide support.

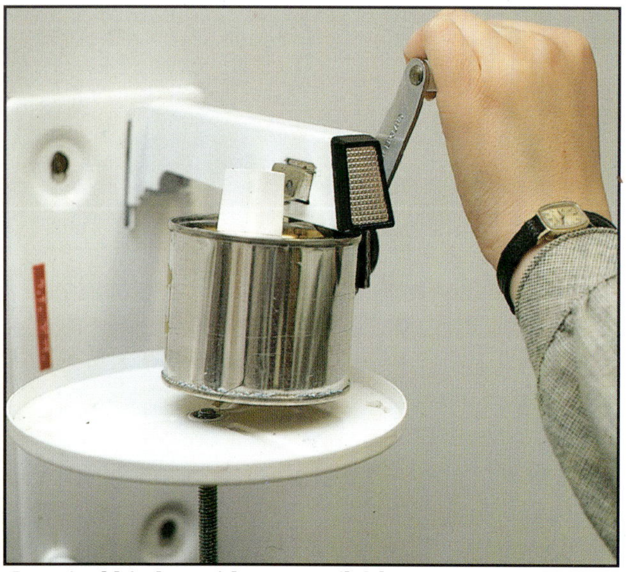

Practical kitchen aids are available.

Stairs need not be a problem.

New technology for paralysis

An inability to move the legs and/or arms presents its own set of problems. Fortunately, in this age of ever-advancing technology, people with very little movement can rely on a whole new range of gadgets based on computers and electronic wizardry. The simplest device is a collar which has two switches on it for the quadriplegic, that is, someone who has all four limbs paralysed. With this the person can start something moving, tell it in which direction to move and use the other switch to tell it to stop. Or they can have a light moving around randomly on a computer screen, stop it on the object they wish to activate and then switch it on with a second switch. This could control all the different appliances in the house, for example, the light, the electric fire, the oven, the front door and the washing machine.

Electric switches of varying size and shape can be made to suit almost any handicap, including only being able to move the head. A quadriplegic mute can be helped to speak by fitting a light beam source to the head. In the photograph below, the boy is wearing a headband which holds a laser. The laser controls a voice synthesizer. By moving the beam across a light-sensitive keyboard which has been programmed to represent words, the voice synthesizer can say what he wants to say.

Modern wheelchairs have become very refined. There are battery-operated electric models which can travel up to ten miles without having to be recharged. They have an all-weather canopy and inside are mobile telephones which enable the driver to summon help if there is a mechanical breakdown.

A disabled man using a voice-controlled computer

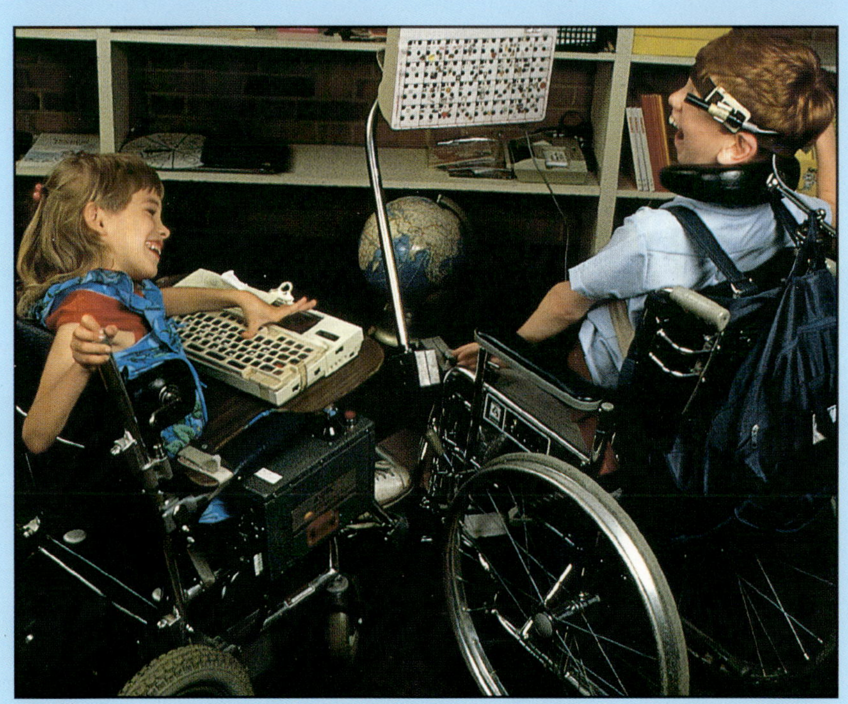
Handicapped children talking with the aid of a voice synthesizer

As the photographs on this page show, various pieces of equipment can be linked to accommodate a handicapped person's disabilities. In the photograph above, the man in the wheelchair is using a voice-controlled computer. This is linked to the robotic arm in the centre of the picture, which can turn the pages of the book.
Many paraplegics and quadriplegics have made the most of modern technology in order to overcome the limitations of their handicaps.

Out and about

There are few reasons why the physically handicapped should not get away from home, to work and enjoy life like anyone else. Physically handicapped people do find jobs for themselves, and can sometimes return to their former occupation after a disabling accident. Alternatively, there are rehabilitation centres where training for different careers can take place. If this is not possible or the person concerned is not able to get out and about to that extent, there are day centres run by local authorities or voluntary organisations.

There is an increasing number of public places displaying the sign shown below. This symbol indicates that there are facilities available for the handicapped. In places such as these, everyday necessities like shopping for food or visiting the bank are now possible.

Hobbies and recreation are also an essential part of normal living. Playing selected games, gardening or studying new subjects can be rewarding pastimes. A local Citizens' Advice Bureau or library will have all the necessary information.

Studying music or art can become more than just a hobby since it offers a chance for personal expression and achievement. There have been many instances where severely handicapped people have turned to the arts and created an extraordinary career for themselves.

Car stickers allow disabled drivers to park close to public places.

Wider check-outs at supermarkets provide room for wheelchairs or walking frames.

Wheelchair ramps are now provided in many places.

There is the National Anglers Council in Peterborough that has useful information for disabled fishermen and -women, and there is a National Association of Swimming Clubs for the handicapped. RADAR (Royal Association for the Disabled and Rehabilitation) has lots of leaflets and guides to shops, restaurants, hotels and public buildings. They have information about London Underground stations, access to London cinemas and hotels (see left) and even a list of suitable public conveniences in England and Wales. The National Trust has facilities for the disabled to visit many of its properties. The British Tourist Authority will help with holidays. RADAR has published a guidebook called "Holidays for Disabled People", which may also be useful.

Paraplegic Olympics

During the Second World War, Dr (later Sir) Ludwig Guttman, a neurosurgeon, was asked by the British Government to set up a spinal injuries unit at Stoke Mandeville Hospital near Aylesbury. He encouraged his disabled patients, mainly soldiers, to take up and enjoy sport for the sake of their health and morale. The response was so good that later the British Sports Association for the Disabled was founded. Now there is a nationwide network of sports clubs. Every year the national wheelchair games are held in a specially built sports complex at Stoke Mandeville. That is, except in the Olympic Year when disabled athletes of the world meet at the Paralympics.

Disabled people participate in at least 46 different sports including parascending, subaqua and ballooning. At the last Olympics in 1988 in Seoul the U.K. sent many sportsmen and women to compete. There were 4,000 competitors from 61 countries. The opening and closing ceremonies were like those of the main Olympic Games. 70,000 people came to see the opening day. The games were very competitive and of a very high standard. They lasted for ten days.

The events competed in included athletics, swimming, discus throwing, high-jump, air weapons, goalball, judo, archery, basketball and table tennis.

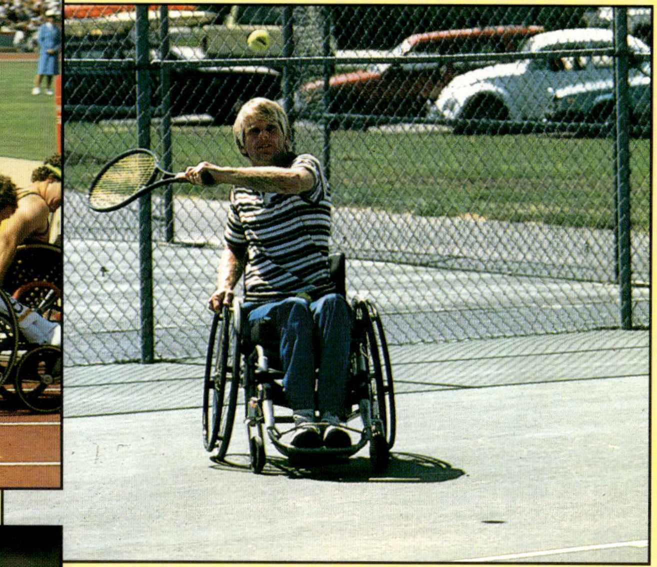

PARALYMPICS

These Olympics aren't just about winning games. The competitors meet fellow paraplegics from many different countries. They are invited to people's homes in the host country. The people from the host country see how disabled people cope with their handicap and excel at sport. It gives their own physically handicapped hope and something to aim for. During the games, there are lots of activities and parties. These games, like the able-bodied Olympics, spread friendship between all the countries taking part.

CARING FOR YOUR BODY

Everyone needs to look after their body. We need a varied diet with the right amount of carbohydrate, protein, fats, minerals and all the vitamins. We also need plenty of fresh air and exercise. But in the same way that we need to exercise our bodies, we also need to make sure that body and mind work together.

At school we need to develop as many interests as possible. Art, crafts, music and dance are just as important in life as mathematics or history and languages. Learning to play a musical instrument, studying ballet, painting, pottery or model building will teach our bodies how to coordinate movements. Good coordination can help us avoid many accidents.

We also need to protect our bodies against infection, so it's important to be vaccinated against whooping cough, polio, tetanus, diphtheria, German measles, mumps and measles. Regular medicals will detect the early presence of handicap.

Sunshine and exercise are good for everyone in the family.

Fresh fruit and fresh air help keep us healthy.

A healthy life-style

The body has to be prepared for the risk of infection and the danger of accidents. A healthy, varied diet with well-balanced meals is what is required. Hamburgers, and sweets are acceptable provided the diet as a whole is balanced. Children especially need plenty of calories because growing uses up a lot of energy. Foods such as cereals and potatoes are a good source of energy. Eating fresh fruit and vegetables, as well as protein in the form of lean meat, fish, eggs, dairy products or pulses gives the body the nourishment it needs and improves resistance to disease. An illness in a poorly nourished person might cause a disability, whereas in a healthy, robust body its chances of doing any real damage are greatly reduced.

Exercise strengthens your bones and develops your muscles. It also refines coordination and improves your general health. Exercise makes the heart grow stronger so the blood flows more effectively round your body. If you have been injured, it will mean that everything heals a little more quickly and easily.

A lot has been written in recent years about the benefits of exercise and a healthy diet. It should also be remembered that smoking, eating too much and drinking alcohol are not good for our health.

Accident prevention

Since car accidents are a common cause of physical handicap it makes sense to take as many precautions on the road as possible. Buy a copy of the Highway Code and make sure you know the rules. Cycling proficiency training helps children learn to use the road correctly. This includes learning how to handle a bicycle and learning hand signals to tell others what you intend to do. Remember, if you are out on your bike at night, wear reflective materials.

Safety belts, restrainer seats, or properly attached carry-cots should always be used in cars. Children should never play in cars as it is possible to accidentally release the hand-brake and this might send the vehicle rolling out of control. A reversing car is also a danger as children are often too small to be seen in the rear mirror.

Young children should always be supervised in playgrounds. Outdoor play is full of risks – climbing things, particularly trees, is one of the joys of childhood, but this always has to be done with great care as it can be dangerous. All in all, the principal ingredient in accident prevention is to simply stop and think. Most of us know very well when we are taking risks.

Cycling courses reduce the chances of accidents.

Seat-belts have prevented thousands of serious injuries which could have led to physical handicaps.

Being cautious

There are many childhood diseases which can cause serious handicap. For instance, polio can paralyse arms and legs. Here is a short list of some others: mumps can cause deafness; measles may cause brain damage; T.B. (tuberculosis) can leave serious lesions in the spine. The risks from all these diseases can be prevented or greatly reduced by immunisation. We are extremely lucky to have all these effective vaccines. Yet, in some areas, only 50 per cent of parents bother to have their children vaccinated. This is sometimes due to a lack of proper health education. Parents should consult their family doctor if they are worried about the risk of side-effects which certain vaccines may involve. These risks are often outweighed by those of catching certain diseases.

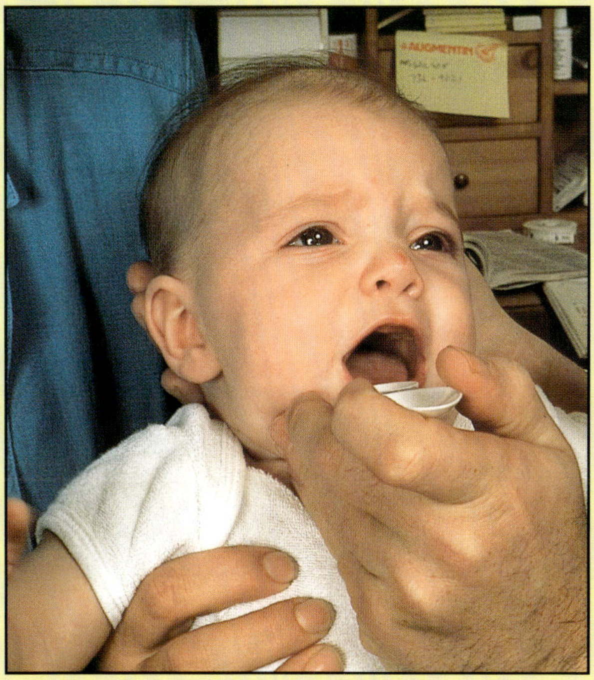

Vaccinations should begin in a baby's first year.

Changing attitudes

In the last ten years the general public's attitude towards physical handicaps has undergone some changes and improvements. This is largely because disabled people were not prepared to just be thankful for whatever was done on their behalf. Most of them want to participate in society as fully as possible. To do so their handicaps must be accommodated.

Laws have been passed in Parliament which provide facilities for the disabled. Most public conveniences have at least one unisex toilet for the disabled. The same applies to theatres, cinemas and hospitals. Local Authorities are spending more money on modifying homes, with ramps for wheelchairs, stair and bathroom fittings. Much has been spent on specialist educational facilities for cerebral palsy sufferers. Electricity Boards have specialist advisers for the disabled. British Telecom will provide loudspeaker telephones for the deaf and jumbo-sized push buttons for those with arthritis. Industry has new gadgets which improve the quality of everyday living for disabled people.

With the help and support of friends and family, the physically handicapped can lead a full life.

PEOPLE TO CONTACT

Association for Spina Bifida and Hydrocephalus (ASBAH)
22 Upper Woburn Place,
London WC1H 0EP

British Rheumatism and Arthritis Association
6 Grosvenor Crescent,
London SW1X 7ER

British Ski Club for the Disabled, Corton House, Corton, Nr Warminster, Wilts BA12 0SZ

British Sports Association for the Disabled
Harvey Road, Aylesbury, Bucks HP21 8PP

The Disabled Living Foundation
380-384 Harrow Road, London W9 2HV

Haemophilia Society
PO Box 9, 16 Trinity Street, London SW1 1DE

Multiple Sclerosis Society
25 Effie Road, London SW6 1EE

Muscular Dystrophy Group of Great Britain,
Nattrass House, 35 Macauley Road,
London SW4 0QP

National Osteoporosis Society
PO Box 10, Barton Meade House, Radstock,
Bath BA3 3YB

National Spinal Injuries Centre,
Stoke Mandeville Hospital
Aylesbury, Bucks.

RADAR, The Royal Association for Disability and Rehabilitation
25 Mortimer Street, London W1N 8AB

Spastics Society,
12 Park Crescent, London W1N 4EQ

GLOSSARY

Atheroma – Fatty substance which is deposited in the walls of arteries.

Auditory nerve – The nerve that carries electrical signals from the ear to the brain.

Axon – Part of the nerve cell through which nerve impulses travel away from the cell body.

Caliper – A metal rod strapped to the leg to support the joints.

Chromosome – Part of cell nucleus which is responsible for heredity.

Clubfoot – A malformation of the foot in which the forefoot is twisted or mis-shapen.

Dendrite – A fine, hair-like part of a nerve cell that carries impulses towards the cell body.

Dendron – Part of the nerve cell that carries impulses towards the cell body.

Diabetes – A disease caused by lack of insulin in the body.

Down's Syndrome – Collection of clinical signs in a person who has one too many chromosomes. It used to be called mongolism.

Embryo – The stage in a developing foetus from conception to the eighth week.

Foetus – The baby in the womb.

Haemoglobin – Red pigment in the blood which carries oxygen.

Heredity – The passing on, from parent to child, of characteristics such as eye colour, hair colour, etc., through the chromosomes. Some diseases, such as muscular dystrophy, are hereditary.

Immunisation – The process whereby immunity is induced in the body by introducing bacteria or viruses in small quantities.

Immunity – Resistance to a disease.

Inflammation – Excessive heat of a part of the body, with pain, redness and swelling.

Macular – Refers to the area of most distinct vision on the retina at the back of the eye, the macula lutea, or "yellow spot".

MMR Vaccine – Vaccine containing mumps, measles and German measles bacteria and viruses.

Nucleus – The central control area of the cell; it contains the chromosomes.

Palsy – Loss of control or of feeling in the muscles. *See paralysis.*

Paralysis – Loss of power of motion, or sensation, in any part of the body. *See palsy.*

Paraplegic – A person with paralysis of the lower half of the body.

Quadriplegic – A person with paralysis of the whole body.

Sclerosis – A hardening of part of the body by fibrous tissue. In multiple sclerosis, patches of thickening appear throughout the central nervous system, resulting in various forms of paralysis.

Spasticity – A tendency towards violent involuntary muscular contractions.

Synapse – The connection between different nerve cells.

Thrombosis – Process whereby clots of blood form in the blood vessels.

INDEX

Photographic Credits:
Cover: Network Photographers; pages 8, 12, 18 top and 24 top and left: Biophoto Associates; page 10: Hutchison Library; pages 14 all, 15 both, 16 both, 18 bottom, 19, 20 both, 21 top, 22, 23 middle and bottom, 25 both, 27 left and right and 29 bottom: Science Photo Library; pages 17 top and middle, 26 top and 29 middle: Roger Vlitos; pages 17 bottom, 24 right, 26 bottom and 27 bottom: J. Allan Cash Library; page 21 bottom: ARC/ Greenleaf Advertising; page 23 top: Janine Weidel; pages 28 top and 30: Topham Photo Library; page 28 bottom: Robert Harding Library.